CALLINGS!

CALLINGS!

Sixteen men and women ponder the jobs they *do* and what they believe they are called to *be* in the world
...and the difference between the two!

Edited by
James Y. Holloway
and Will D. Campbell

PAULIST PRESS
New York / Paramus / Toronto

Most chapters in this book were originally published in the 1972
Fall-Winter issue of *Katallagete,* Journal of the Committee of
Southern Churchmen, Nashville, Tennessee. © 1972.

Copyright © 1974 by
The Committee of Southern Churchmen

Library of Congress
Catalog Card Number: 73-90070

ISBN: 0-8091-1806-8

Published by Paulist Press
Editorial Office: 1865 Broadway, N.Y., N.Y. 10023
Business Office: 400 Sette Drive, Paramus, N.J. 07652

Printed and bound in the
United States of America

Contents

"Callings...?"

James Y. Holloway

James Y. Holloway is the editor of *Katallagete: Be Reconciled*, the journal of the Committee of Southern Churchmen, and teaches at Berea College, Kentucky.

It would be fair to say that the work on this book began before the Committee of Southern Churchmen was organized and began to publish *Katallagete*.

One of the objectives of the Committee and the journal is to voice consequences of confessing "Jesus is Lord" we do not find articulate in mainline Christian institutions. Had we not been convinced that something essential to the Christian faith was missing from the faith and order of these institutions, we would not have been trying to say what we've been trying to say these past few years. At one time or another, many of us had been on the payroll of the Church as professionals. The rest of us would have served within the framework of their programs had our experience been other than what it had been. But we shared a conviction that mainline Christianity was losing its birthright; specifically, that it had surrendered to the world the very matter which lies at the heart of the Gospel and which is the subject of this book, the calling of those who confess Jesus as Lord, the vocation of those who do not but who believe that life means something other than what they do on their job. Some of us found it difficult in our calling as Christians to distinguish who we were and what we did from the social workers, administrators, political appointees, lobbyists or technicians required by any institution in our society at the end of the twentieth century. In other words, it was not the Christian "laymen" as car salesmen, business executives, machinists or football players who seemed indistinguishable from the world in their "calling"; it was we, the "full-time" professionals of the Church. And this seemed to us the surrender of our birthright as Christians.

No one questions the validity or the necessity of social work, administration, education, politics, science: everyone is against hunger, misery and ignorance wherever it injures the family of man, and everyone supports efforts by political and social activities to ease these burdens which have become increasingly heavy on an increasingly large part of mankind. What bothered us was the fact that our calling as Christians into the world had become only one more effort to tend the world's sicknesses and wounds using the world's diagnoses and remedies. That seemed to us to deny that the calling of the Christian into the world is something distinctive; the point, say, of Jesus' parables (which, the record shows, not everyone understood or accepted), or of the correspondence of St. Paul about the place of the Christian in the world.

Those who follow Jesus' call seem, by these New Testament accounts, to be different from the world not by their goodness and morality—that is, not by what they do or say—but by who they *are* by the gift of God in Jesus. Disciples, as is well known, are called to be *with* and *for* but *not of* the world. It is Jesus' call to disciples which defines "the world" they are destined to serve. The disciple cannot be *with* and *for* the world if he is not thereby called "out" of it, so that he may know where the world is and what it is doing, and thus bring to it the Word of life which judges and overcomes its slaughters and lies. Yet our Christian institutions and professionals (which included many of us) seemed indistinguishable from the world by our words, deeds, goals: we were using the same methods to achieve the same goals which we measured in the same way the world did. It was as if there were no stories in the Gospel about lost sheep, good Samaritans, salt losing its savor, children of light, and the good works and intentions which finally brought about the execution of Jesus.

Vocation, *calling* by God to the world, is not about a "reformation" of the Church, about "bringing the Church 'home.'" Maybe there never was a "reformation" of the Body of Christ because there was never a need for one. Maybe the only "reformation" in fact, in history, was the *conversion* of the Church into a minion of the State, of Caesar, beginning in the fourth century and continuing unbroken unto now. That conversion of the Church to serve the politics of the various Caesars who have since appeared does require a periodic reorganization of the work of the Church to keep it apace with the culture and values of the particular Caesar which rules at a particular time. But this reorganization has nothing to do with "reforming" the Body of Christ; it is only a fresh "conforming" of the Church to the world, and specifically to the State. In fact, how is the Body of Christ "reformed"? Jesus was no "reformer"—religious, social, political; nor were St. Paul or the prophets who spoke to our fathers of old. When Caesar converted the Church from life in the Lord to life identical with the world, "reformation" became a periodic, necessary and characteristic work of the Church: St. Benedict, St. Francis, Luther, Calvin, the World Council of Churches, Vatican I and II, National Council of Churches, Consultation on Church Union. Such "reforms" were neither prophesy nor the Word of reconciliation given by Jesus in the Gospel. They were and are, however, "reformations" which enable the Church to keep abreast of, relevant to and thereby indistinguishable from the world, the State, Caesar.

Hence the suspicion that the institutions of the Church today are in a Babylonian captivity as complete and as blasphemous as the captivities opposed—but only in "reformations"—by St. Benedict, St. Francis, Luther, Calvin, WCC, Vatican II, COCU. And a captivity of the character and nature of our own times; one that places the Christian in combat with "flesh and blood," not against the "principalities and powers" of the technological society. It is once again Dürer's interpretation of Ephesians 6:10-17 in his "Knight Between Death and Devil." Could it be that the Church, its institutions and professionals, are as determined by the techniques which rule our society as the White House, ITT, Yale University, the Pentagon, and any other business, educational activity or music and sports? Should we not therefore refuse to enlist in Norman Mailer's "armies of the night" which march on the Pentagon and elsewhere for the same reason that we should not join movements for "church renewal" via ecumenism, political activism, social relevance and refurbishing the liturgy? So long as the Christian continues to identify the Body of Christ with the way any institution must of necessity organize in order to exist in the twentieth century, his efforts at "reformation" will inevitably result in only one more adjustment of the Church into a more appropriate harmony with the world. And are not such movements of "reform" in fact and in deed, sociology and administration, and not theology? Are they not works, devoid of faith? Should we not, with Jesus, St. Paul, Amos, Isaiah and Jeremiah, attack only the "doctrines" of the Church, and leave judgment on her "morals" to the sociologists?

A year or so ago we decided to take these misgivings about the professions and institutions of the Church as a point of departure for an issue of *Katallagete*. Over the years we have come to know a lot of folk who had experienced the same misgivings. Moreover, there was another and related matter that made it necessary and easy to talk with those outside the Church who knew the same frustrations and agonies of trying to make sense out of life in the professions and institutions of the twentieth century: no longer possible was a simple identification between what one did to earn a living and what one tried to affirm about life's meaning. Vocation was not necessary to job.

But many of us, Christian or otherwise, had assumed without hesitation that the liberal, middle-and-upper income "professions" were clear and unambiguous vehicles to serve mankind. If Christian, then within the institutions and agencies of the denomination; if humanist, in secular, especially political and educational enterprises of social concern and "outreach." Our Church heroes (*not* the figures called by God as recorded in the Bible) seemed without exception to have been from one of the professions. But some of us have experienced in our lives the transformation of these Dr. Jekyll professions into the perversions of the Mr. Hydes of the technological society. Physician, lawyer, minister, teacher, priest, scientist, politician, administrator and the divisions and subdivisions thereof—each seems trapped by what institutions and professions have been turned into by technique. Concern for one's fellow man through profession or institution is transformed into the dehumanizing goal of contemporary technology: efficiency. The transformation has nothing to do with good will or mischief. There is no conspiracy to debase mankind that can be laid to Roosevelt or Stalin, Goldwater or Mao, the Kennedys, Nixon, Dr. Spock or Fidel Castro. Devils driving out the good demons which on occasion inhabit our souls cannot be exorcised by a change of political party or ideology, a victory of the revolutionary movements of the poor led by the intellectuals, or Youth Evangelism using all the techniques of mass persuasion identical with Sunday afternoon professional football games. After all: what is the difference between the organization of any major religious denomination and the organization of any insurance company, conglomerate or university; between Woodstock, Expo '72, "Easy Rider" and the Democratic National Convention? The issue is neither to indict nor demean the Southern Baptist Convention, Joe Namath, Frank Mankiewicz, Peter Fonda or ITT. The issue is to call attention to the fact that the work of each is hostage to, indeed, defined by what Jacques Ellul has painstakingly described as contemporary technique.

Not only or even especially has the assembly-line worker described in Charlie Chaplin's "Modern Times" had his very soul and being transformed into a gadget by what he does "on the job." It is all of us, most especially those of us in the educated, middle-and-upper income professions. We are the ones who have been indoctrinated *by our training* to believe that "education" will be the sure guarantor against being debased like the assembly-line worker in "Modern Times." The technicization and institutionalism of our society make it impossible to serve mankind-in-our-neighbor following the liberal "professions-as-vocations" for the same reason that the factory worker in Detroit or Dayton, Ohio cannot serve God or neighbor at the assembly-line. So where is the dignity of labor in modern times? Physicians have thrust between them and patients their medical school, drug and medical supply houses, the American Medical Association, the College of Physicians and Surgeons, Blue Cross-Blue Shield, Medicare, hospital regulations and procedures, labor unions —all of which are united for efficiency, but first and last render physician and patients into objects, integers, items. After all, what physician or patient could do without any one of those services which define the efficiency and the character of modern medicine? And so lawyers, ministers, social workers. And so teachers: their early training in public schools, then in the university, graduate and professional schools, then their teacher associations and guilds, administrators, trustees, registrars, deans, chairmen, faculty committees, accrediting associations, tenure—all unite to block the dialogue between the student on one end of the log and Mark Hopkins on the other. On his side, the student moves into the "higher" reaches of education disenchanted with the conformity exacted by his entire school experience, cynical at what the great teaching machine of contemporary society imparts in both public and private actions, mesmerized by the media so that he can learn only by pictures, movies, slides, comic strips, TV (reading and dialogue are alien and hostile "materials and methods"), suspicious that even the young and hip professors are after little more than to use him for their own purposes. It is one Object using another as Object, in this instance, indoctrinating it, adjusting it to the society which is in fact a system— perhaps education is where Western civilization today most closely approximates Ellul's projection of technique easing us into "a society of objects, run by objects." And yet, it is no one's "fault." No one is to be blamed, except for ignoring the signs and realities of what is happening to us.

Strange that the Bible pays no attention to what a man does to make a living and instead shows interest only in the *call* from God. We read about "religion and the rise of capitalism" and "the protestant ethic and the spirit of capitalism." We were taught that Jesus calls men into *"full-time* Christian service" and that these professionals must remind the *"part-time"* Christian laymen that honesty in business affairs, chastity outside his own household and regular church participation makes their lives as sincere as the lives of the "full-time" professional. But the Bible neither teaches nor reads this way. We do not know much about what the prophets or apostles did part-time to earn a living in a job or by a profession because it is not important to their *calling* from God. Amos dressed sycamore trees; some of the apostles fished commercially; John the Baptist foraged (but made no demands that soldiers or taxgatherers do likewise if they wanted to "flee the wrath that was to come"); Micaiah ben Imlah was on his government's payroll; David could do (and did) most anything. But that about exhausts our information on their "part-time" jobs. What they did as a job was not integral to their *call,* their *vocation* which was given from God. Any one of them might just as well have done what any of the others did as far as job was concerned. God's *call* was not a call to work for a living part-time and for Him part-time. Some jobs abuse the neighbor and are forbidden by God's call: witchcraft, for example, and the professions and careers that rob man of his humanity (slavery, violations of the sixth commandment; in our day, drugs, no doubt). But work is *not* vocation.

For some of us the question of work and vocation today is a matter of witness and catacombs. It is the importance of the words of St. Paul to the Christians who lived in Corinth: *When anyone is united to Christ,*

*there is a new world; the old order has gone, and a new
order has already begun. From the first to the last this
has been the work of God. He has reconciled us men
to himself through Christ, and he has enlisted us in this
service of reconciliation. What I mean is, that God was
in Christ reconciling the world to himself, no longer
holding men's misdeeds against them, and that he has
entrusted us with the message of reconciliation. We
come therefore as Christ's ambassadors. It is as if God
were appealing to you through us: in Christ's name, we
implore you, be reconciled to God.*

The vocation of the Christian as *ambassador,* as
witness, has first and last to consider well what God *is*
in Jesus: that, and that alone, is God's call to those
who confess Jesus as Lord: to be ambassadors of, to
testify, to witness to what God has already done in
Jesus. That is *all* that Christians are to be or to "do" as
Christians. To witness to what God does for all men in
Jesus is *all* that a Christian *is* as a Christian. Nothing
more? *That,* and nothing more. Jobs—yes, pumping
gas, farming, student, selling hardware: as Ellul reminds
us, St. Paul's warning that to eat one had to work is
the consequence of living East of Eden. To work is
our condition as human beings—but it is an especially
fragile condition today, for Caesar (the State) determines not only where and how most of us work, but
whether some of us will even be permitted to work. If
Caesar decides we don't work, we don't, and our lives
(to be more accurate, the lives of those society defines
as "minorities") are literally in the palm of Caesar.
Such is the true significance of debates about "full employment," "welfare reform" and "job opportunities"
and it is a witness that most Christians today ignore
because *the world* finds the message of Revelation 13

illiberal, intemperate. To control work the way the State controls it in any advanced society today is to risk the State of Revelation 13.

Being a Christian is no simple matter. That is why it is *being,* and not doing, that occupies so much of Jesus' attention, and Paul's. It is always simple to do allegedly "Christian" acts in a specific cultural situation: the kinds of sex licensed by the State (though not necessarily the same as the amusements of those who control the State); certain kinds of charities (concerning the poor, the ignorant, the minorities); certain kinds of piety ("belonging" to a religious organization —not necessarily to God; pulling beads; circumcision; tithing; committee serving; no loitering in hometown bars; good credit ratings; "well-thought-of" in the community), etc.

But the vocation of witness to Jesus is not so simple as "doing" anything. It is a matter of the new being God gives in Jesus. It is not a matter of the works we do which Caesar warrants or encourages. Anyone, *anyone,* can do "Christian" actions warranted by the State. Few are *called by God* into the vocation of being a witness to the Lord (or to anyone else, for that matter). One thinks of the recent witness of the government of the United States (and its witnesses) in the Courthouse in Harrisburg, Pennsylvania. What divided *true* witness from false witness was not what either set of witnesses did or had done. Those in the docket "did" nothing by way of witness in that courtroom. What divided true from false witness was who the witnesses *were.* A witness is credible by who he *is,* not by what he "does." Consider, in this encounter at Harrisburg, what the government of the United States of America "did" as witness in that case, and who the other witnesses *are*. The credibility of the witnesses to what God does in Jesus comes not by what the witnesses do or have done, but because of who they *are* by the gift of God.

And this takes us back to the abdication of the call of God by the Church. Our generation is especially guilty of the false witness of social action and pining after relevance to the world by identifying with cultural enterprises and election politics. Our liberals seek to engage the Church and its institutions in every situation the liberal world has already defined as a "crisis": certain (but certainly *not all*) wars; ecology, racism, etc. Our conservatives seek to prove the Christian "answer" to everything their world defines as a threat undermining its system: drugs, pornography, sex, petty thievery, etc. But let the world of either liberals or conservatives shift its interest or its fears, and the witness of the Church shifts with it, and calls the movement "reformation." Small wonder the witness of the Church to the world concerning almost anything about Jesus lacks credibility in the very world Jesus came to seek and save. It is the false witness of the Church which proclaims that God is Dead and Caesar alone lives because Caesar alone is doing something.

Our professions as our institutions are indistinguishable from the world we were called into as witnesses to what Jesus does for it. How can we serve the world if we *are* the world—participating in its errors, a party to its deaths? Our schools train the men and women of the Church in professions which employ the same devices and techniques that Caesar's schools must use, and therefore the outcome is the same for both. Christians thereby sanctify the world's death grip on mankind, and bear false witness to the Lord of Eternal Life. Our scholars and theologians are as tough-minded, professional and objective as the professionals whose image they seek to recreate in themselves. One thinks of the recent and celebrated "International Council of Learned Societies in the Field of Religion" held in Los Angeles, and the indictment against it by a fellow scholar and black brother: an "affront" for "no African or American black scholar appeared on the program," even on the panel concerned with "theology and culture" which included a dozen "theologians." "I cannot conceive of any set of reasons except indifference, insensitivity or racism that can explain the omission of black theology or African theologians. . . . I do not think it unfair . . . to conclude that the planners of this conference and the so-called liberal academics in the field of religion have no profound and abiding interest in black culture and religion, even as a problem, and no real appreciation for the scholars, white and black, American, European and African, who write on these issues. The failure about which I write must be understood not only as a failure of individual persons but of religion as an academic discipline. The learned societies seem to be as racist as any corporation subsidiary in South Africa or Angola. The Los Angeles meeting demonstrated that the dominance of white racism has not yet been ruptured in religious departments and theological seminaries." These words of Dr. Preston Williams of Harvard University appear not in *Mohammad Speaks* but in *The Christian Century*. Not for the scholars of the contemporary Church is the Credo *imitatio Christi*, but *imitatio mundi*. Our training for the profession of ministry (teacher, scholar, minister, priest, administrator) denies that Christians are *called* by God, set aside to live in the catacombs of the world and away from its scrumptious feast-tables and salons, filled with intrigue, licentiousness and the delicacies grown and harvested by the flesh of human slaves. The *vocation,* the calling of the Christian, is to witness to the world about that Word made flesh for the sake of the eternal life of the children of the world. Vocation is not to witness to one another as fellow professional Christians. The goal of our professional training would seem to be the replacement in the White House of Father Mc-Laughlin, S. J., with a minister whose social ethics approximated those of the Americans for Democratic Action; to replace Dr. Kissinger with a "Christian" doctor of political science and international relations. But the false witness that desires to make changes such as these is the same false witness which preaches toading sermons in the East Room, makes hard-boiled speeches at fund-raising banquets to Re-elect the President, and coordinates international policy to fit domestic politics. When it comes to the matter of Christian *vocation,* what is the difference between Billy Graham and Bob Hope, or for that matter, Henry Kissinger? In other words, it is II Kings 22 all over again.

Schooled in that kind of witness, with such goals laid before him, what has the "teacher" of Christianity to teach? In specifically Christian institutions of higher education, the order has long since been reversed so now education is evangelized with the same enthusiasm and for the same reasons put forth by Thomas Jefferson and the Department of Health, Education and Welfare. Education is what is Good about the News. This is a rejection of the clear message of the Gospel that trusting Jesus is not a matter of learning "something" in order to "do" something. It was not Jesus, but Socrates, who identified knowledge with virtue. And for a fact, it is Socrates, not Jesus, who is the Lord of most institutions of higher education which identify themselves as Christian. Perhaps the replacement of Jesus by Socrates took place in the fourth century, not in the nineteenth and twentieth. But this does not alter the fact that Christian professionals utter blasphemies and live in heresy when they teach "something" about Christianity that is "good" for their students to know, because Socrates proved that if one knows the "good" he will "do" it—everyone wishes for his own good and will get it if only he can find out what it is. That sort of wisdom is the genius of Socrates, but it is not the Gospel of Jesus. As Kierkegaard put it, it is the difference between a genius and an apostle.

Small wonder, therefore, that there is an increased interest in the Socratic sort of Christianity-as-ideology whenever and wherever the foundations of the world are shaking and its values are rotting. So we should expect more Christianity as something to be "taught" and then something to "do": that is, more Christianity-as-ideology using the vocabulary of the Bible and the sit-down comic style of Shelley Berman; more of the Gospel according to the funny papers; more quarterbacks for Christ because they are quarterbacks, as we already have more singers and generals for Christ because they are singers and generals. Such movements are in fact only weak reeds which try to prop up institutions and professions in cultures which are doomed. And such movements are building into an especially tragic episode for young people who once again will experience what it means to become the victims of a rip-off by the same generations that used civil rights to keep down blacks, economics to keep down Chicanos,

Vietnam to test military and social science techniques, and the whole system of law and government to assimilate dissent from the values of the majority culture. Movements today of Christianity-as-ideology which proclaim something to "know" in order to have something to "do," are middle-and-upper income trips because one must have the leisure and financial resources to participate in *any* movement in the twentieth century. The only "movement" the poor can work in is a struggle for survival. So in large measure the movement of Christianity-as-ideology—as all movements—feed upon the helpless and powerless identified as minorities by the world.

The fact is, one cannot "teach" Christianity in these, or in any circumstances, and he ought to beware of trying. The distinction that the New Testament treasures between evangelism and education can be made clear, and made to prevail in the classroom. The metaphors and examples can be used which emphasize that distinction, even the hyperbole of Jesus' parables. A life—even perhaps lives in a few communities—can *be* the truth that Jesus is not a matter of knowing "something" in order to do something to merit reward, a good grade, a diploma, a recommendation, a job. Such parables, especially the parable of a single life, can demonstrate that what is good about the news in Jesus is that it is not something that can be "taught" or even "demonstrated." The good news is a *call,* a vocation from God.

So the call of the Christian is not necessarily a true witness because it is exercised as a job in a certain institution or a particular profession. In fact, the call of the Christian may have everything to do with what the Christian does *not* "do" but with who he *is* in any institution or profession.

About this volume: considerations such as these led us into a consideration of work and vocation in the twentieth century. We asked some people we know to help us spell out some of these and other consequences about job and calling, work and vocation, by reflecting on their own experiences. The selection was meant to be neither representative nor thorough. We were not after a theory of vocation, since that seemed beside the point, especially so in the twentieth century. Instead, we asked some people whom we believed had something to say from their own experiences to write about the question of jobs and vocation. Some we wanted (and who themselves wanted) to write for us could not: their vocation had led them to prison where they are forbidden by Caesar to share their experiences with us, even by the public, written word.

In sum, we asked these folk to reflect on their own experiences about their jobs, their professions, their work and how this related to what they were trying to be and to say about the life they believed they had been called into.

That is what this volume is about.

Work and Calling

Jacques Ellul

Jacques Ellul's most recent books to be published in the
United States are *Hope in a Time of Abandonment, Au-
topsy of Revolution, The Politics of God and the Politics of
Man, False Presence of the Kingdom* and *The Meaning
of the City*. Earlier works include *The Technological Society, Propaganda, The Political Illusion*. He is Professor of
Law and Jurisprudence at the University of Bordeaux and
an active member of the Reformed Church in France. The
present article was translated by James S. Albritton.

I

It is not necessary to undertake a lengthy study to realize that nothing in the Bible allows us to identify *work* with *calling*. When the terms that can be translated by the word "vocation," or "call from God" are encountered, they are always concerned with a summons to the specific service of God: a summons to be prophet or apostle, but also king, as was David; and eventually, to serve God by an exceptional act, without even knowing one is serving Him, as the Chaldeans, or Cyrus, or the king of Damascus. It is never a question of work—with the exception of Hiram and the construction of the Temple. Work is (we cannot, of course, produce a "theology of work" within the limits of this article!) a natural exercise of activity which either places man in a positive relation to the creation (the situation in Eden), or in a negative one (in the rupture with God, and "East of Eden"). In the latter case, work becomes painful and compulsory in the attempt to survive. In any case, however, it does not represent a service to God. It is an imperative of survival, and the Bible remains realistic enough not to superimpose upon this necessity a superfluous spiritual decoration.

Moreover, the Bible is not essentially concerned with this situation of work. It is the common and distressing lot of everyone, but it is not particularly important. It has often been noted that one can find hardly anything in the Old or New Testaments about how the Judges or the Prophets, the Apostles or the Disciples, earn their living. The references to Amos the shepherd, and Paul the maker of tents, are exceptional indications of little consequence. It has often been said that this lack of reference was due to the fact that on the cultural level, in the Jewish and then Greco-Roman worlds, work held such little place and importance (and this is not certain) that people did not speak of it—and not because *it should* have little importance before God. Biblical detachment in this respect would then not be normative. In reality, however, this observation is without substance. For if work was conceived as a calling, a vocation coming from God, the Bible would have accorded it an importance that it may not have had culturally. In addition, one should ask why it was desirable to extricate from the Bible the idea of work *as* calling, at a time when work was becoming important, culturally?

When Christianity became dominant in the Roman world, about the third century, certain theologians began to put a high value on work. This coincided with the political movement: the Empire had more and more need of workers and manual labor. This is not, however, the principle point. I do not at all believe, in this case, the Marxist interpretation (which is valid, on the contrary, for the use made of Christianity by Western bourgeoisie during the nineteenth century; we shall speak of this later), which states that the theologians formulated an ideology of work-in-the-service-of-God, *in order to* induce people to work conscientiously, with serious minds, without deceit, etc. Rather, the idea of work as vocation, as calling, appears to me to derive from two perspectives which progressively emerge in Christian theology from the third to the fifth century. The first arises from Greek philosophy, and is what I would call the passion for *unity*. The ideal life is *"One,"* undivided, just as the ideal for the Greek city was unitary organization. All philosophy is oriented by this attraction to the *One*. The world is bad because it is shattered, divided, separated. The *One* is both the reversion to the original situation, and the fulfillment of all convergencies. Man must establish a life of oneness, unequivocal; he must not be divided. Under these conditions, and for faith, it is evident that God is the essential part of our life. It is a function of grace—the Word which is revealed to us—and faith, that unity should be constituted. Man should be of God and for God—in all that he does and in all his works. His life is not made up of incoherent and successive moments, but is one in the recapitulation of Christ. Likewise, man's diverse works are not thrown to chance: they form a whole with respect to the grace which has been given by God. Consequently, each one of these works is related to God; and, moreover, they come (if one is faithful, if one is a believer) from the will of God: recognized, discerned, accepted, loved. There will be a calling, a vocation addressed by God, not only in His service and in accordance with the proclamation of the Gospel, but also for the "states" we adopt: a vocation for marriage or celibacy, for example. Therefore, there will be a vocation for work and even for a particular work. This is what is required for our lives to be *One* in God.

But there is a second motive. We have just spoken of a calling to the service of God. Yet, more and more during the fourth century, this service to God appears not only as preaching, in the service of the Church, "deaconry," etc., but as a service in the world through the idea of Providence. God wills that the world of His creation survive. He wishes to maintain it. There is a certain order of the world which is willed by God. Hence, all that we do to maintain Creation itself (make it last; have children, work), and to preserve its order, is a service to God. Thus, military service in the fourth century could become a calling because it was part of the maintenance of the worldly order willed by God. And, or course, work, labor. All of this appears to me to be clearly formulated during the fourth and fifth centuries. However, these theological constructions will be wiped out during the troubled period from the fifth to the tenth centuries.

Then, during the Middle ages (tenth-fourteenth centuries) a more confused situation occurs. During this period, there is in reality two contradictory currents. For some, work is purely and simply a curse, a sign of the condemnation of Adam. Consequently, it does not possess any value in itself and cannot be the object of a calling. Genuine vocation is expressed, for example, by the acceptance of poverty, and the tendency toward the begging monks (the mendicants) which corresponds to this idea. At the extreme, some will say that this world is a place of evil, dominated by the Princes of this world: we should do all in our power to speed up its end. Here, Catharism unites with a certain Christian orientation. One must do nothing to make the world last; on the contrary, to seek to bring about the kingdom of God is to work for the end of the world (from which the Cathars based their refusal to procreate). But one also finds among the theologians the contradictory tendency: the defense of the ideology of work—its sanctifying value, its integration into the unity of life, and consequently, the idea that God calls us to perform a specific work. Yet, different sorts of work are distinguished. Agricultural work is sanctifying, and can be the object of God's calling; it is a service to God in Nature. Contrawise, commerce, and more so, money traffic, is not susceptible of incarnating a vocation from God. Generally, all the theologians who attempted to construct dogmatics during the Middle Ages encountered the problem of work and energetically resolved it in the direction of a choice made between work which pleases God, and work which is damnable, and in the affirmation of the unity of man's life, entirely submitted to grace, man is called upon through these works to attest to that grace. Work was not excluded; it was the object of a vocation God addressed to man. However, it concerned more a universal, as opposed to an individualized, calling.

The situation will be reversed during the fifteenth and sixteenth centuries, first of all, by the great movement of secularization which began during the fourteenth century, and again, by the development of economic activities (and especially commerce) which tended to set a high value on work. Work subsequently becomes both more essential than in the preceding period, and it finds itself "ennobled." The idea of work as a curse slowly disappears. During the fifteenth century, one begins to find the argument, so often developed during the Reformation and the eighteenth century, of the uselessness of the monks (and especially the begging monks), because they do not work, and produce nothing. Work begins to be (what it was not in the thirteenth century), a value as well as a virtue.

It is amidst this cultural climate, this psycho-economic mutation with respect to work, that Martin Luther appears. He cannot reject everything that has taken place. The society in which he finds himself works as never before! The social category he principally speaks to has made work the end and meaning of life. Only the view that *everything* is related to God, that *everything* comes from God, is retained. Thereafter, work is also related to God. Work is validated, but this is true only because it comes from God, because it is a part of the order He established for man. Thus, Luther will forcefully argue, in the celebrated text about the cobbler, that in making shoes, the cobler serves God, obeys his calling from God, quite as much as the preacher of the Word. At times, during the Reformation, the idea that work is a service to God through man also appears: the worker renders services to other men and, in doing so, obeys God's commandment.

It was also necessary to consider another interpretation of calling: work could be dreadfully painful, crushing, and mortifying, but such was God's will. It was necessary to assume this burden, this condemnation, to accept it, because it came from God. Thereby, one rapidly arrived at a concept which would be developed during the seventeenth and eighteenth centuries—that of work as redemption. It is obvious that this was part of man's vocation, man's calling. However, an important change takes place. Luther had heavily insisted on the individual character of grace, on the singularity of each calling. Could that which was true in the spiritual realm be false in the temporal—if one served God in the one as well as the other? Hence, he who performed a particular profession did so because he was called upon by God to hold *that* particular profession, and not another. Each individual entered into God's design in a particular way. There is no longer a *general* calling for work, but a unique calling addressed to such and such individual to become a bricklayer, or a doctor, etc. This brings about, on the one hand, the impossibility of thoroughly classifying the professions which please God, and those which are cursed (God calls a particular man to a particular work . . .). On the other hand, the individual assumes the responsibility that each person must ask himself: what type of work does God wish *me* to do? And this will arouse the uneasy conscience of Protestantism—the uncertainty concerning the obedience to a call which is never so obvious as to leave no room for doubt. In any case, all this results in a tremendous professional conscience. It was clear that he who acted by vocation should place all his zeal, all his love, all his strength, in the service of God. The economic consequences which this would have for the development of capitalism and the bourgeoisie are very familiar also. It produced a considerable valuing of work, and we then see its development through reciprocal influence: the more work is valued through the idea of vocation, the more economic activity is increased; and, conversely: the more economic activity is developed, the more work is valued.

In the ideological realm, this question takes on a double orientation. On the one hand, work is lifted to its highest pinnacle of exigency and concrete value by the bourgeoisie. We are all familiar with the "commonplaces" which resulted: that, for example, "he who works, prays" (which comes directly from the confusion between work and divine calling). Or, even, "work is freedom," emphasizing the redemptive character of work. We also know about the use made of God's will by the bourgeoisie concerning those who work. The bourgeoisie employed all these religious ideas during the nineteenth century to maintain the workers in submission and obedience to a divine order. At this time, the call to work (vocation) becomes once again collective, and a means of exerting social pressure, while, within the bourgeoisie itself, the sense of vocation as a personal service to God through a profession (often liberal) is very often maintained. This implied the display of exceptional qualities: one worked with more passion, taste, and care, because one worked for God and by His command.

It is also necessary to underline the other aspect of the evolution of the idea of work as calling—found in the writings of Karl Marx. Marx lifts the ideology of work to its summit. Man is what he does (in his work). Work *is* what distinguishes man from the rest of nature, so he awards work an exceptional place and virtue. Hence, Marx gives us this admirable text concerning the result of work:

In your use of my product, I will directly enjoy the consciousness of having satisfied a human need and objectified the essence of man, of having been for you the Middle Term between yourself and the human race; of being known and felt by you as a complement to your proper being and a necessary part of you; thus to know *myself* confirmed both in your thoughts and your love; to have created in the individual manifestation of my life, the manifestation of your life; to have therefore formed and realized directly in my activity . . . my human essence, my social essence.

Such is work according to Marx. And one can see how greatly he is influenced by the idea of vocation in his condemnation of the capitalist system—which destroys through exploitation the eminent and constructive role of work! This prodigious, high value of work, argued by Marx, which before him, had never known such exaltation, is the result, on the one hand, of the growth of work in the Western world during the nineteenth century, and, on the other, the secularization of the idea of man's divine vocation in work.

II

Now, it is clear and obvious that, with the evolution of our society, it was impossible to maintain such an ideology of work. [Assuredly, it still exists and some try to make it endure: for example, Herzberg, *Le Travaal et la Nature de l'Homme* (Paris, 1972), but it is an attempt which is condemned in advance!] Of course, one can say whatever one wishes on the philosophical level, but it has become very clear that nothing, in any historical epoch, could justify any such idealism of work. Since the nineteenth century, we have witnessed the degradation of work in three stages, yet we must always emphasize that it is never by glorifying the work of the artisan or the peasant as being easier, less tiring, etc. There was, perhaps, in this latter conception of work a greater possibility of confusion with God's command. On the one hand, the crafts represented a more individualized type of work, directly implying the rather personal idea of service, and the accomplishment, or creation, of a product expressing all the personality of the author: one could see if the product was a success or failure. It was a more complete type of work, at the same time subjected to the rhythm of the worker himself. Similarly, the peasant works in nature, and inevitably, the medieval idea was preserved that Nature, as the natural environment of man, is good. Work which is done in nature is "closer to God." (It is not, however, a question of work which is more agreeable.) These two aspects which encouraged the confusion between work and calling, have apparently disappeared, and we can now observe the shattering of the unity between the two terms, work and calling.

First of all, there was capitalism. With wage-earning, work becomes a commodity which is bought and sold. Man is then dispossessed both of his power to work and the product of his work—in exchange for a salary which allows him to do little more than survive. This salary absolutely does not represent the true, superior, "transcendant" value of work. On the contrary, it reduces work to *nothing more* than a commodity. The individual whose work is sold in this manner can have no initiative, no joy; work can no longer be the expression of his personality, since he has no other objective than to produce the objects which will enter into the commercial circuit. Hence, it was from this time already difficult to maintain the idea of work as calling, as vocation. The situation will be further aggravated, however, as the age of the machine fully develops. The problem is now familiar. For example, in the works of Georges Friedmann: *"Le travail en miettes"* ("Work in pieces," "atomized work"), and *"Où va le travail humaine?"* ("Where goes human work?"). Work separated from workmanship has become pure and simple obligation without any meaning—shattered through division and specialization. The worker is ignorant in the end of what he does and makes. What is the utility, the value, of such work? He is also ignorant of the materials with which he works and is familiar only with the gadgets and instruments—thanks to which he works. The atomization and fragmentation of work prohibits any understanding of the activity to which one devotes oneself. Specialized professional training encloses the worker in a narrow sphere of activity. Personal reflection is no longer possible concerning the "how" of his work. There is a rupture between thought and action. And this leads to the situation where each action of the machine's servant will be calculated by a third party, who is specialized in the "man-machine" combination, as well as in the combination of the machines among themselves, in order to form a harmony among them. From that moment, man's work is entirely subordinated to the possibilities of the machine and to the necessities of the organization of machines among themselves. This is represented, for example, by the problem of "cadences" and the Taylorization process. This means that work, from which man is now totally dispossessed, can be only an activity alien to him, imposed in some fashion from the outside. Work can no longer correspond to any inward reality, and literally holds no place in the true life of the worker—and yet it absorbs the major portion of his lifetime. Under these conditions, it is obvious that work could no longer be a vocation, a calling. Of course, it is always possible to contend that God can transform the worst situation, and that He can restore the sense of vocation to the worst type of work. But this really represents a convenient refusal to see the real situation: Work such as it is today cannot be universally upheld as a calling. At best, let us say that God can by grace and miracle cause work to be lived by man as a gift and a calling. Nonetheless, the *theological* rapport between vocation and work has been broken: work as such is not vocation, not a calling.

Today, the general technicization of society has even aggravated this rupture. Technique has become the mediator between all actions and all intentions. In our world, it is necessary to depend upon techniques in order to accomplish anything at all. And furthermore, technique has its own specific quality of efficiency; in fact, efficiency is technique's major characteristic. Consequently, technique itself destroys any recourse to added efficiency. Where true technique exists, it is not possible to employ Amroise Paré's formula: "I dress his wounds, and God heals him." It is not possible to say, "I pressed on the accelerator, and God made the car speed up." This regularity of effects, this specificity of means, this generalized intercession of technique, leaves no room for the concept of vocation as calling. Quite to the contrary, we know there is serious criticism of "calling" in the technological society: where a strict technician is needed, one cannot accept a man endowed with vocation, or God's calling. Possessing vocation becomes a means for *not* becoming a competent technician. We are all familiar with men who present themselves for positions as professors, educators, psychologists, because they are obeying a calling from God to a vocation—and are perfectly incompetent. Even more so, we consider that even for a specialist, vocation can cause much bungling in the use of technique: a nurse who obeys her vocation will let herself be influenced by sentiment in her work, and no longer be dominated by the rigorous criterion of efficiency. We also know what this social, pedagogical or medical work becomes in the absence of "calling": the application of cold techniques, the radical indifference of the practitioner toward his patient, the exactitude of the gestures in the absence of human relationships, the transformation of the patient into a case, a number.

Now, all of this results from the generalization of

technique-as-mediation, which makes any grafting of vocation to technique impossible. It is only in an abstract and theoretical fashion that one can say: "There is a vocation, a call from God, and he who received it becomes a perfect technician." Or, "Beyond the use of a perfect technique, there is the marvelous adjunction of God's gesture in calling us to vocation." All such thinking is simply romantic idealism. In reality, it is perfect technique which excludes the very idea of vocation. There is only one fact to remember: technical efficiency permits us to treat a greater number of "cases." But: one cannot indefinitely multiply human resources with resort to pity, sympathy, compassion, love.

This radical rupture between work and calling, due to the "capitalism-machinism-technicization" trio, has caused as a consequence, the crisis of calling among Christians themselves. I would like to look at this crisis from three angles. First of all, it has become well known (at least in Europe) that the theory of vocation has often become a way not to pay for services at their true value. Just as the bourgeois made workers obey by explaining that their condition was the fruit of the vocation which God had given them, so in many Christian and churchly enterprises, "vocation" is used as a pretext to give lower salaries (and sometimes no salary at all) to nurses, social workers, pastors, teachers, etc. "Since you obey a vocation coming from God, you're not really going to demand to be paid for obeying an order coming from God!" This speech, made by the presidents of businesses and churches in Europe, facilitated things for them very well! At the present time, of course, there has been the expected reaction to it, and these "servants" now demand a salary equal to those who fulfill—without any calling from God—the same function. But as a consequence of all this, vocation itself has become suspect. When a professor or a tutor hears the words "calling," or "vocation," his reflex is "Well, they are invoking my 'calling,' and that means they are not going to pay me what is just and fair for what I do." So even serious Christians frequently want to hear no more of vocation—for they consider it as a means of blackmail.

From a second point of view, calling as vocation is under a shadow with Christians due to the fact that the Church's responsible people (pastors, etc.), feel very much debased in a world of technique since they are not themselves specialists, and especially not technicians. To obey a calling and then to preach, to direct a congregation, to take time for soul-searching—all this seems frivolous in a world of engineers and producers. So, these embarrassed pastors also want to become technicians. They therefore practice psychoanalysis, group dynamics, social psychology, information theory, etc. And it is as psychoanalysts that they will act upon the Christian community—no longer because they were called upon by God for service. Here again it is totally illusory to believe that technique is simply added to, or serves, vocation: technique *in fact* substitutes itself for vocation.

When we combine these first two criticisms of vocation by Christians we rapidly arrive at the third: the refusal to admit that there can be any calling from God to render a vocation of service to the Church. In other words, Christians have fallen into precisely the opposite error which characterized the old identification between work and calling. Now, there is no longer any vocation in being a pastor or a deacon. It is simply work like any other work. The young French pastors have pushed this to the extreme: "We work in an organization which is the Church; we are ordinary wage-earners (thus a proletariat), used by a boss (the Church) who is like many other bosses. We make use of techniques (biblical exegesis or preaching—both having become pure techniques). In all of this it is not a matter of vocation, of a choice coming from God. . . ."

This denial of any possibility of vocation expresses not only the normal consequences of the process of technicization of society, not only the politization of the thinking of the young pastors, but especially the fact, very hard (although unconsciously) felt, that it is no longer possible in our society to incarnate a vocation concretely. If there is a call from God, we must find a way to express it, that is, to incarnate it. But this has now become practically impossible. So calling, vocation, tends to remain something purely inward, purely spiritual. Yet for a faith centered on the Incarnation, this is simply not acceptable. It represents a total divorce between what society unceasingly asks of us (work, military service, etc.) and God's will. Service to God cannot be written into a profession. But where then? Faced with this impossibility, one can understand the reaction: it is easier to shed oneself of the concept of vocation, of the idea that there can be a calling directed to us by God. Everything is simplified if we retain (even in the functions of the Church) the purely social and technical aspects, while rejecting all the rest. So after having unified work and calling by absorbing the professions into vocation, Christians again unify them by excluding vocation, which today has become impossible. Our situation at present, consequently, is that we find ourselves torn between work which no longer has any significance at all (and which brings no satisfaction to man) and calling, which no longer finds any possibility of incarnation.

Under these conditions, what are the possible responses if we do not accept a pure and simple rejection of vocation, if we continue to believe that *God* calls us to fulfill a particular *service?* One attitude that is still frequently adopted consists in saying that, fundamentally, there are still certain professions which can be conceived of and lived as God-given callings: physicians, to heal and preserve life; lawyers, to defend the poor, the widows and the orphans; teachers, to aid in the formation of character; psychologists, social workers, etc. . . . Christians could, therefore, direct themselves toward these professions. But I am sure that this is in no way an answer to the question of work and calling. In the first place, these "bourgeois" professions imply that Christians must be part of an "elite." Again, it is a complete illusion to believe that these professions are any longer peculiar vocations for Christians. They have become as technical as any other profession, and professional exigencies rapidly efface the sense of calling. And finally, these professions can more often than not be seen to function mainly to reintegrate our technical society. Thus, to become a lawyer by "calling" represents the expression of good sentiments, a generous will, an idealism, but it means in reality to be the victim of an illusion and to live in ignorance of what is real in our society. In our times, there is no "profession-vocation."

Therefore, we might move on to another answer: we must accept the fact that work is condemned in our society; that there is a segment of our life which is "cursed." Hence, we can abandon ourselves to a trade or profession which is without any value, without any significance, without any interest, which functions solely to supply us with enough money to survive, and we shall find the main interest for our lives elsewhere. This is the attitude of all those sociologists and social psychologists who believe that man is going to find the good life in leisure: Let us accept the fact that we shall not be living while we work. It will be rather a sort of lethargy, a blindness, an unconscious sleep (and especially let us not even approach consciousness). We shall be aroused by leisure, where we shall become ourselves at last. At least we shall live. And so it shall be exactly the same with respect to calling. Vocation will be a part of leisure, whether one undertakes some search for Christian life in his spare time, or whether one divides, traditionally: "The week for the world, Sunday for God." This dichotomy facilitates things very well! One can be an efficient and ruthless businessman for six (five!) days; on Sunday the whole of the Christian calling is resolved through participation in worship, Church festivities and works. But it is obvious that this is not satisfactory, and it is unnecessary to linger too long upon it. The case against "Sunday Christians" has often been made. But, neither must we forget that we cannot bring "a little Christianity" into modern work. It is simply out of the question to adopt the attitude often held by the Catholic Church: to bless "externally." That is to say, to Christianize by adding a little prayer or benediction to professional activities. One's work will never be transformed because, at the beginning or the end of it, he prays to God for several seconds. Moreover, there can be a complementary form to this hypocrisy: to imply that the obedience to a God-given vocation is to live as a Christian whose calling is seen clearly and is manifested in his exercise of a profession; that in the style of a Christian in a profession, there would be an incarnation, and not merely the addition of a few pious words.

So: we have established our powerlessness. What then can we say?

III

The first observation we must make is that, on the ideological level, work is of the order of necessity. It is given to man by God as a *means* of survival, but it is also posed as a *condition* for survival. This is evidence which St. Paul emphasizes: If a man does not wish to work, then neither shall he eat. It is not, therefore, a part of the order of grace, of gratuity, of love, of freedom. We must always avoid confusing the two when we speak of work and calling. At this juncture, I am repeating what I wrote concerning violence. For like violence, like political power, work also is part of the order of necessity. One cannot escape it; it is the human condition resulting from the rupture with God. And let us not forget that even after the Incarnation and Reconciliation, we still remain men. We have not become angels. We must still eat to live; we are still subject to the "necessity" of growing old, and we are still subject to the final necessity, to die. In Christ there is no suppression of the order of necessity: there is victory over that order. Victory of the Resurrected over death, of the Crucified over the powers of this world, of love over evil. But death, evil and the powers of this world still exist, and they form the order of necessity by which man is always trapped. Work is a part of this order. At no time, and in no circumstances, can one say that from a Biblical point of view, "work is freedom." It is just the contrary. Human experience encounters just this revelation in Christ, and that revelation never beguiles us with illusions. So, we must accept it as we have been given it. And we should especially not pretend it to be something other than what it is. Otherwise, as Pascal remarked, "He who wishes to play the part of an angel, plays the part of a beast." Consequently, we must *also* accept work as calling, but not at all as a calling to live like a Christian, as being redeemed, as being free. On the contrary, we must accept it as a calling to recognize ourselves as *creatures* (finite, limited, submitted to necessity) before God, as *sinful* creatures (suffering the consequences of our rupture with the Father). Work should be received in faith, marked with this double qualification. Consequently, it is "normal," in that it is alienating, overwhelming and insignificant. We should accept the feeble stupidity of it as being the mark of the absurdity itself which constitutes our lives. Therefore, work has no ultimate value, no transcendental meaning. Before God, it is that which allows us to survive and which characterizes us as human beings. This realism matches our earlier observations, and suggests the destruction of bourgeoise or Marxist romanticism, as well as any idealism concerning work.

However, the recognition that we are in the order of necessity does not at all imply the scorning of work, or the refusal and criticism of it: such is indeed the order to which we belong, and nothing more. The only thing which is forbidden us is, precisely, to confuse the order of necessity with freedom—which is to say, *grace;* which is to say, *vocation.* Work is completely relative before God. After the criticism of work by Ecclesiastes, all of the sociological studies about work are quite vain! There is no place for illusion about work. Work does not lead to anything decisive. Particularly in opposition to Marx, work does not constitute the essential meaning to life. Work is incapable of giving meaning to life, or of shedding light on what man is, or of leading to truth. We must accept the fact that while working we are truly in the most completely relative type of situation. This is what is meant by the expression: "Sufficient unto the day is the evil thereof." Work is thus limited in everyday life, and even limited to the banal, to the "hopeless." It is neither value nor creation. If we receive satisfaction from our work, like the doctor who cures or the artist who creates a work, we must not then say: "such is the *true* measure of work, by which we must measure all other tasks, that of the poor assembly-line worker, or that of the wretched laborer." No! It is in fact the latter type of work which is more genuine. And when human endeavor produces joy, or produces a work which seems to surpass the ordinary, then we must be conscious of an exceptional event, a grace, a gift of God for which we must give thanks. If we consider work in this manner, then we join realism with Biblical discernment, and we cut the wings from the idealism concerning a marvelous future where each person will do rewarding and significant work.

On the other hand, however, relative work is not without value and interest, since it also allows the possibility of continuing on in life, of maintaining the world, and consequently it opens up the possibility of history. Here, Marx's interpretation is fully valid: it is obviously work which allows history to be made. And this is

God's will. Hence, at this level only, there is vocation: God calls us to a particular work (whatever it may be!) to prolong this world, which He has not yet decided to terminate and to judge. It is an entirely relative task, but it must be done. I will say it once again: it is not because something is relative that we should disdain it. Christians are all too thirsty for absolutes. What is relative never interests them (from which proceeds, for example, the many political errors they commit). Now, it ought to be otherwise. That which is relative should concern Christians, for the absolute is God's affair. It is in the domain of the relative that we should be engaged, precisely as Christians. The relative should be considered as our true place, and should be taken altogether seriously from now on: "If you have been faithful in little things. . . ." This, however, excludes the decisive importance of the choice of a profession, as the idea of calling, in the sense we have discussed it in the above pages.

If it is not in work that we can unify our lives, or even incarnate our Christian vocation, if the society of technique brings us back to the hard condition of relative work, without ultimate value and significance, then it is obvious that we must discover a form of activity which expresses our Christian calling, which implies an incarnation of faith. And since we are involved in this world, it cannot be a purely interior matter, nor a work in the sense in which that word is usually taken—for example, in "work of charity." The Christian calling should be expressed in an *activity*—in an activity having a social and collective "impact," susceptible of modifying in one way or another the shape of the world we live in, and an activity that can only be gratuitous, while preserving the characteristics we usually attribute to work: seriousness, competence, continuity, invention. It seems to me that it is in this manner that activity can express vocation, calling, for the Christian. But since this calling is gratuitous, an expression of grace from God, activity should in response also be gratuitous. It should serve to help the men who surround us to live and society to endure. It should, therefore, be an equivalent to work, but also, a "plus," and consequently, perhaps, bring meaning.

I would like to give an example, taken necessarily from my own personal experience (but not in order to promote myself as an example!). I undertook—and this could represent a response to my own Christian vocation—work in a "Prevention Club." We so call an organization whose goal is to respond to the call and need of young people who are usually designated misfits: former beatniks, hippies, young toughs, runaways, drug addicts, rebels without a cause, delinquents and pre-delinquents, etc.; in other words, those who have maladjusted behavior in all its forms, and especially, suicidal behavior. It is not, however, a question of either locking them up or giving them medical treatment. They should simply have a chance to find a gathering place that they like, and where they can come simply because they find it congenial. They should be able to do things they like to do, with good friends. Therefore: no obligation; no pressure. Secondly, it is not a question of making them "normal"—that is, making them conform to the model society would make for them, or adapting them to some kind of work. It is, in fact, a matter of giving them the means to transform their *negative* lack of adaptation into a *positive* lack of adaptation. This means helping them learn about their personality so that they can change negative behavior into a capacity for innovation, their aggressiveness into a force of controlled action, and that they themselves develop the capacity to face the difficulties in their lives, and integrate their tensions into fruitful efforts. This is done, first of all, through certain activities (parachuting, mountain-climbing, scuba-diving, sail-boating, etc.,) during which they learn control and team relations, for these activities should always be dangerous enough to represent a genuine challenge. Secondly, an effort is made through open, interpersonal relations, which one can call "psychological therapy" if one wishes, but which has never had the character of a rigorous application of psychological techniques. To direct such an enterprise like the one I have described (and, of course, this includes a full-time, therefore, a paid staff) is genuine work. But to the extent that this does not fall into the realm of *necessary* work, as society sees it—since it takes for granted a large autonomy of action, unceasing innovation, and free choice—it appears as being truly related to the personality of the individual who is involved in it. This seems to me to be an example of one of those possibilities of incarnating grace, in a specific and unconstrained manner. I find some meaning in this. However, it implies that each person seek and invent an activity of this nature, and not be reduced simply to copying what is already taking place somewhere else. This is always the great problem with all Christian "works" for if we have received a calling, a vocation, to live in this world as witnesses, it involves us first of all in the initiative of that incarnation which can never be repeated.

Do we not, however, find ourselves again in the situation and difficulty we have encountered earlier—the division of life into two separate parts, the one devoted to work without value, and the other valued as a calling? Is this not in reality a solution of despair? To be sure, it contradicts the idea of the Christian life as the unified life, integrating the totality of our actions and feelings. But we have seen that this is not necessarily the authentic Christian understanding of life. If we have understood the true place of work according to the Scriptures, then we should not be distressed by the fact that our Christian vocation does not fall in the domain of work. Nevertheless, work is not the "cursed part" of our lives—the part which presents no interest, which has to be endured while awaiting vacation-time. In reality, we must assume, accept positively, and take upon ourselves, this sign of our rupture with God— to live fully this order of necessity, *in order that* the freedom which is at times granted by God, the calling which we are able to assume, represents *its* true value. It is only through work, not as calling but as constraint, that the vocation which is incarnated in a work of gratitude takes on meaning. It would be disastrous to think that while I am occupied with the Prevention Club I am obeying God, while the rest of my time is anonymous, without interest or significance. I should rather be convinced that it is also working at something without significance that I am fulfilling God's plan.

Christian living thus presents itself as a dialectical movement (not dialectic that is a type of *reasoning,* but a movement of *actual experience*). What is devoted to constrained and insignificant work represents negativity: this is actually the negativity of calling, the inverted image of vocation, the expression of the impossibility of living it, of assuming it, of incarnating it. This inverted image must exist, in order that, on the one hand, we know fully what compromises vocation, and on the other, we are encouraged to express it. Calling exists. Work in the modern society of technique shows us the certainty that such work is not our Christian vocation. But this should not in any way stop us, as the "discouraged soul." On the contrary, we should seek out what is possible as incarnation and accomplishment by beginning with this negation. And conversely, when we have discovered what form vocation could eventually take, when we have invented the "how" of concrete evidence, then, the work we are obliged to do to earn our living should become enriched, valued, and to a certain extent, significant.

Thus, these are not two separated parts of life, but two faces of the dialectical movement. We are not actually dealing with a stable and kept situation, but with a relation that is constantly being challenged, a progression which results from the influence of the one on the other. And in this process, the negative portion always has a *creative* function—due to incessant questioning and re-questioning, which constantly obliges me to seek out the most satisfactory incarnation of my calling. This consequently implies that there should be a certain relationship between the two—that the choice, the invention, the discovery of the vocation form must have something to do with the work accomplished through necessity. It is obvious that if I am a doctor by necessity, and consider my vocation to be found in boating, there will be no such relation. In this example, the second choice cannot make my work significant, since it is of the order of leisure, and not vocation (which means it is of the order of false sociological freedom, as opposed to true freedom, which is grace and gratuitousness).

If I take once again the example of the Prevention

Club, I would say that a professor who is called upon to deal with students, but who does so only because of professional requirements, could express his calling by taking care of young people who are different from the students, and by situating himself in another set of circumstances. But what he would then learn through working with young misfits could lead him to discover a whole facet of his students that he would not have seen as a professor. He is then engaged in a new relationship with them. Certainly, work would still remain coercive and necessary—with the typical sluggishness of institutions, the absurd regulations, the meddlesome and unjust authorities. But he would find himself removed from the function of a professor and into a total human relationship—not by humanitarianism or by liberalism—but by the effective discovery of the problems of young people. Reciprocally, the negativity of the professional function teaches how one should *not* deal with young misfits, just as the negativity of university organization instructs one as to what should not take place at the Prevention Club!

Each person must consequently choose the form of the incarnation of his vocation with respect to his place in the order of necessity. However, this implies a reversal on our part as to the manner in which we can conceive our lives and our relation to society.

In summary, I will say that calling no longer concerns what we had so long thought it did—an entry into an order (of life, of the world) willed by God as such, and to which one adheres by vocation. Rather, calling is an entry into a *disorder* (although apparently "ordered") established by man, and this disorder will be upset and put into question each time we seek to express our calling.

Comparative Demonology

James G. Branscome

James Branscome is a staff member of Highlander Center, New Market, Tennessee, and a former director of Save Our Kentucky, an organization opposing strip-mining in Kentucky. He is a member of the Editorial Board of *Katallagete*.

Since I read Thomas Merton's article a few years ago in *Katallagete* on contemporary Christian "snake-handling," *viz.*, the more destructive tests of faith involved in blessing missile rattling by the established church as opposed to that of mountain folk who do a more simple test with rattlers, I have been particularly interested in comparisons between the mainline churches and their agencies in the Appalachian mountains and the indigenous churches of the hollows. Not that I have gone about trying to find folk who still do the more simple things like handling copperheads; it's just that Merton's discussion of the subject excited in me an interest in what might be called comparative demonology. The study is a casual one, involving mainly chronicling the acts of professionals working in the mountains in the name of Jesus Christ and their Mission Boards and comparing their fury to that of less pious Christian mountaineers doing things that interest them.

I have never worked out a rating scale of one to five for the study, but I do have a few prejudices against which various acts may be calibrated. One of these prejudices centers around an obscure German named Frank Overbeck, whose English statements are contained in some paragraphs in the writings of Karl Barth and a recent issue of *Katallagete*. Overbeck says simply that anyone engaged in assigning the term "Christian" to anything—history, vocation, work, state, etc.—is engaged in an act of blasphemy that obscures Christ and subjects the "wholly other" to the chaos and relativity that is peculiarly man's on this side of eternity. In his view most Christian utterings from the Patristic Age forward have been "satanic." About those who make their utterances in more studied fashion, he says: "Theologians are not the advocates but rather the gravediggers of Christianity."

Another prejudice comes from Jacques Ellul's

writings, especially *Propaganda*. This one is to the effect that the most easily fooled (propagandized) people, the ones most suspect of having been seized by the myths and commonplaces of modernity, are well-schooled Christians. Or to state the same another way, I have a prejudice which says that the greatest threats to Caesar are those *not* schooled in "overthrowing" him, analyzing him, or generally going about trying to amend his worldview. Those who know the larger scheme, and thus see merit in "both sides of an issue," are less likely to be "swimming against the stream" or engaging in any action that distinguishes their activity from that of the average energetic liberal or conservative social activist.

While comparative demonology is not yet a science, I defend it against those who would claim that it is necessarily a subjective, emotional endeavor reflecting only the prejudices of its practitioners. To disprove this notion I offer a case study involving some low-churched people down in the Sergeant York country of the Cumberlands in Tennessee. A few years ago some local poor people, mainly of Cherokee and Choctow breeding, were supporting themselves by supplying rattlesnakes to a local white congregation which used them in their ceremonies. According to one of the Indians, this church group was quite fervent. In his words, "They were a bunch of holy-rollers who threw them snakes around to each other every night, jumped benches, and just generally hooped, hollered, and raised quite a shine." Since he lived near the church and was a Christian himself, he was quite disturbed by all this. Finally, he says, they got so loud one night that "they was bothering my poor mother. So I took myself a few good drinks of moonshine, loaded up my pistol, and went down there and told them they were serving the devil, that the good Lord wouldn't have anything to do with their sort." For this act of concern, the Indian got seventeen counts of disturbing a church worship brought against him by the church members and had to leave the county and move in with a group of blacks in the Mississippi bayou. While admittedly this Indian's mission was nothing like a letter to Christians in Corinth, or anything like that, it was a move that deserved better consideration than it got. If I had a scale, I'd give the Indian a plus one and the holy rollers a minus five. After all, the resort of the church people to civil authority to handle one of their brothers in Christ, especially one who attempted to call to their attention a matter of grave concern to him about their behavior, signifies their continued recognition of the State (Caesar) as the best arbitrator of even those affairs which exclusively concern Christians.

There is a vast chasm, however, between the snake-handlers who use Caesar as an occasional resort of convenience, and the mainline church people in Appalachia who make matters of Caesar their *total* resort, who would have nothing to do or say if Caesar's administrators did their jobs as well as the church bureaucracy believes it does its job. For example, about two years ago when I was working as an employee of the Appalachian Regional Commission in Washington, I was confronted—almost accosted—by two churchmen from the Methodist establishment who ran volunteer programs for the church in Appalachia. What the two were so excited about was their insistence that they had found the "model" volunteer program for sending folks to work in the mountains. Unlike Vista and the programs they had heard I was involved in, theirs was different: it *reconciled* people. And to back up their claim, they produced a diagram spelling out exactly how a volunteer "facilitator" was to go into the mountains, make contacts, and follow all the other steps that led finally to reconciliation. They had come to ask me, as one of several bureaucrats they were seeing that day in Washington, if I could help them fund their program for reconciliation. The only thing that distinguished these men from any Vista or Peace Corps bureaucrat in Washington was their haughtiness, bred by a seminary education that had confused them beyond the average. No government bureaucrat I ever met claimed that he was engaged in reconciling people through his program, particularly not in the name of Jesus Christ. After checking on the particular "two year demonstration of the model" that these two men were promoting, I found that not a single individual from or in the mountains was involved in the program. The bulk of the money the Church was investing in the program was going to train New Jersey college students in how to appreciate mountain culture, taught in a classroom by a non-mountaineer.

This experience was not an isolated one in Washington. I sat through another session in which the director of the Church's combined mission in Appalachia threatened to turn the Church's Washington lobbyists on the Appalachian Regional Commission if the agency did not fund a "feasibility study" to determine if poor people could run their own cooperatives. The money the Church sought would have funded various denominational economic development experts to carry out the study. The study, of course, was never funded by the agency because it insisted that its own economic development experts could do the same study. To end the Church's insistence in the funding matter, the executive director of the Appalachian Regional Commission finally had to send the group a message to "be reconciled" and think of something to do that the government could not do better.

About a year later I attended a session sponsored by the same church organization on strip mining in the mountains. At the meeting were persons who had been damaged by strip mining—a process of bulldozing down mountains to mine coal from the surface—and a representative of the coal industry which has profited so greatly by this process of coal extraction. After a session in which the mountain folk had described how their homes were being destroyed, their wells polluted, and even the graves of their children dug up—and the industry spokesman had spelled out why this was all necessary to produce cheap electricity—the two church bureaucrats in charge of the meeting pleaded that they be allowed responsibility for setting up further sessions so that "the dialogue established here can be continued." The suggestion was greeted with jeers by the audience, a group that included the Old Regular Baptist preacher Dan Gibson, an 86-year old coffin maker who held the strippers off his and his neighbor's property with a rifle. The church bureaucrats had assumed that it would be possible to get the group to recognize the legitimacy of the exploiter's activity. The anti-strip mining movement has its own theological position on strip mining: in the words of one strip-mined victim, "God never meant for the land to be tore up like it is."; another, "I can think of no greater sin than destroying God's Creation."

This contrast between the established and the hollow churches is typical. The Old Regular Baptist and Primitive Baptist preachers and laymen have tended to be the ones who have led successful campaigns against strip mining, most of them non-violent community efforts that have forced the operators out of the area. These same churches feed more hungry people, visit more sick and imprisoned, than all the combined missionary efforts of the established Church. All without fanfare, program or budget; generally, without haughtiness. Most importantly, without consulting or even being aware of Caesar's efforts to do the same thing on a more impersonal basis. Unlike the established churches, many of the hollow churches in eastern Kentucky deliberately refuse to be subsidized by the coal and gas industry that has exploited so long this area's people and land. Even the Brethren Church—one of the most scrupulous about its investments—gains a large portion of its annual income from corporations that leave behind the human misery of Appalachia.

This list could continue endlessly. I cite some examples only to prove my point of agreement with Overbeck: "To judge from it, Christianity seems as completely abandoned to the world as anything else which exists there."

I find nothing in my own experience that indicates to me that Christian social and political action is in any way unique; that it results in some better "model" for human betterment, as opposed to some purely atheistic "model." The same is true for Christian thinking, Christian magazines, and other Christian prescriptions of one form or the other. For the most part, there is nothing in the best of Christian journals that can rival that of, say, the *Nation* or *New Republic* or *The Amer-*

ican Review, MS., or *Rolling Stone.* Most of all their type of Christian endeavor is just plain boring, following the lead of the secular forces only after all the sex is sapped from the issue. Being a graduate of a Christian college, I know firsthand that there is nothing, absolutely nothing, distinguishable about Christian colleges—except their haughtiness, their dreary haughtiness. It has taken me as long to recover from my college schooling as it did to get it.

These Christian colleges are a clear and definite threat to the region they claim to serve. By draining Appalachia of its most talented, and also refusing to admit those who most need an education, colleges pose a double threat to the region. Those they do educate for so-called Christian "service" are educated to serve the very institutions which I have said in a previous issue of *Katallagete* are in existence to annihilate the Appalachian people. The worst thing about an education, I am convinced, is that it is designed to remove what anger there is in the soul of those it captures. Christian colleges are in business to contribute to the preservation of society without opposing it, without training their students to place a question mark alongside everything that society does, thus blaspheming education and Christ. Christian colleges have contributed to one of the most fundamental dilemmas of modern civilization: it is without the preserving aspects of opposition.

In 1934 Reinhold Niebuhr made the following observation about this dilemma: "Protestant theology in America is, unfortunately, unduly dependent upon the very culture of modernity, the disintegration of which would offer a more independent religion a new opportunity." Ellul has made the following statement of our circumstances in the new age of technology; "Technique, instead of provoking conflict, tends rather to *absorb* it, and to *integrate* instinctive and religious forces by giving them a place within its *structure,* whether it be by adaptation of Christianity or by the creation of new religious experiences. . . . Mankind is no longer in his traditional state of freedom with respect to judgment and choice." Ellul argues that we need a revolution in a world in which revolution is impossible. The insistence of Christian colleges that not even they be opposed, is indicative of how little they comprehend—and therefore can teach about—the techniques to which they are enslaved.

For a time during and after my college years, I felt that there was some possibility of changing these institutions by getting to campuses students who were less well credentialized, less likely than valedictorians to accept and propagate the myths of higher education. I never knew exactly what such a group might do; I entertained notions that maybe they would rise in chapel while the choir was singing an aria and line-out "Amazing Grace" or something, or demand that the college bring in a coal miner to teach an Appalachian Studies course—things like this, small things that "good students" who volunteer to tutor in the hollows on weekends would never think of. It never happened. The few of the right kind of students I saw make it onto these campuses never made it through. A dean would catch them drinking beer and advise them to join the Army or go home. There is no way to out-practice a technocrat, particularly a pious one.

By somewhat of a fluke, I got a job after college working at the Appalachian Regional Commission in

Washington. The fluke was that a foundation sent me up there to learn what was happening to Appalachia and, because I was the first mountain person they had ever seen at the Commission, they hired me to stay. I learned a lot in a year and a half in Washington, not about Appalachia but about bureaucracies. They are fun places, actually. It's very easy to upset a great number of people with little effort.

After a year and a half I learned that there is absolutely nothing that can be done to change an institution like the bureaucracy. You can bring some people in to fight them and before long they will have them on the payroll. It is possible to influence one project here, one there, but the overall effect is nil. As a matter of fact, I now know that the only way to bring down the American government is to take away the bureaucrats' free phone service. Take that away and you take away the great advantage that they have over all reformers and revolutionaries: bureaucrats do not have to pay their own phone bill. If you cannot believe that, remember that the mighty Democratic Party in this country almost went into total demise because it could not pay its phone bill. The winner of the next great revolution will be the one who can first pay the most to AT&T. That's what I learned in Washington.

There are no ways I know of to impede institutions, especially any peculiarly Christian ways. If you are a Ralph Nader and enjoy that sort of thing, it may be possible to make the institutions work better. One in this kind of position is particularly vulnerable, however. There is always the danger that some Democratic liberal will come along and appoint all your lieutenants to the FTC or the FDA. Development of new life-styles is equally dubious. Washington could not now survive without Dupont Circle and its hippies, San Francisco without Haight-Asbury and North Beach. I even have doubts that the mountains can survive the influx of the "new culturists" who have invaded them. Recently I saw the results of such an invasion on one of the uncorrupted sides of the Smokies in Tennessee. Armed with a copy of a design for a geodesic log cabin, a group of these new settlers chopped down a whole poplar stand belonging to a mountaineer because the design book said that only the first six feet of the tree could be used if you had to build the cabin quickly without drying the logs. If this is not what getting absorbed by technique and efficiency is all about, I do not know what is. After a while one gets the feeling that movements are created just so people can get involved in a technological myth for a time, and then reject it for a higher "Consciousness."

At present I am devoting my time to trying to help some mountaineers and conservationists stop the strip mining of Appalachia. If we succeed it will be only because the techniques of stripping for coal in the mountains are less efficient than the techniques for stripping the Western Indian and public lands. It seems to me of some advantage to make this industry's move as quick and unpleasant as possible. There is nothing that makes a Christian any better able to do this work than anyone else.

In my spare time, as I said, I like to keep a notebook of comparisons on what Christians are doing and claiming special blessings for doing in the mountains. If I have a reason for doing this beyond having liked Merton's statement on comparing demonology, it is best expressed again by Ellul: "This is not the hour for

Utopias, nor for political realism: it is the hour for becoming aware . . . (that) Christians are so deeply imbued with the fundamental doctrines of this world that they no longer have any liberty of thought or of life." This thought disturbs me; Franz Overbeck's suggestion that we prepare for the restoration of whatever replaces the present madness of western civilization intrigues me, particularly his insistence that it will be the so-called conservative, fundamentalist, non-crusading church which will be around for the restoration—if there is one.

I know of no way to speed up the process, but a good cheer from the sidelines occasionally is probably helpful. Bothering institutions for light and transient causes, like disturbing your mother, seems to me to be in order when opposing them successfully, for greater sins seem impossible.

I Hear Them...Calling
(And I Know What It Means)

Vincent Harding

Vincent Harding is Executive Director, the Institute of the Black World, in Atlanta, Georgia, a writer and historian who has spoken in universities and at conferences throughout the United States. He is completing a study of Black radicals from the first slave ships to the present.

Callings are strange things. I think I've heard a fair number in my time, perhaps fewer than I was supposed to—or maybe it was more; I'm not certain now. Sometimes they proved to be nothing more than echoes bouncing off from other lives (lives I sometimes thought were mine) and passed on their way. Others puzzled me, and led me into ways I do not yet understand. Some I understand and fear. A few—perhaps more than I know—I have followed as far as they led; and some are still moving. Still moving, preparing to join themselves to the sounds of the new summons, and I suspect there are yet borders to cross.

Callings are strange things. The first I remember (or want to remember?) came through the Black believers who were my extended family in a Harlem congregation. I felt their loving, often demanding grip on my life at an early time—maybe 6 or 7—and heard the call through all their voices and fiercely possessive hopes.

Up there on platforms and stages, at all the church programs, reciting the poems and Bible verses, I heard them set me apart: "He's going to be a preacher," that call said, (really meaning, he is going to be *our* preacher, ours, to assure the continuance of our hopes beyond the borders of our lives) and it was a while before I understood that it was supposed to be *my* calling, that I should hear it and respond.

It took a while for that to happen, for I was hearing other calls as well—or thought I was, though I'm sure I didn't name them that—and was trying to move with them. Like the calling to be an athlete. (This was before Jackie Robinson, so I'm not sure where I thought that road would lead. Perhaps I simply thought that a man should be able to spend his life doing what he really liked, and I liked everything that had to do with balls and bats and running and jumping and falling and feeling the strength of bodies against each other. I liked them far more than the violin and then the piano lessons that my mother hoped in vain I'd like.) That lasted for a while, but I wasn't growing as tall as I thought an athlete ought to be—especially one who thought he was called to play first base, among other things—and I began to hear other calls.

Somehow I got involved with building model airplanes, partly, I suppose, because no one had bothered to mass produce television sets yet (and we probably wouldn't have been able to afford one) and partly because there were no brothers and sisters to share the sometimes lonely days with. That's when the call came to be an aeronautical engineer (whatever that is), and I hadn't found out that Black folks weren't supposed to be aeronautical engineers. What I did find out was that my mathematical skills weren't good enough to pass the test for the high school where all the really bright, aeronautical engineer-types were supposed to attend; so that call too was pressed aside. I think the model airplanes were pretty good, though.

Meanwhile, the loving, tightly gripping community was pressing me forward—not entirely against the sometimes showmanship of my will—into minor church offices, and other responsibilities. And I continued to be up in front at the programs (we, education-oriented folks that we were, mostly of West Indian heritage on the way from Africa, we called them *Lyceum* programs, following traditions of self-improvement deeply instilled in the African people of this country and elsewhere), reciting, only now it was a kind of quasi-acting we used to call Dramatic Reading. That was how I met

James Weldon Johnson and Paul Lawrence Dunbar (not really knowing who I was meeting, not really hearing many things they were calling to me), and Walt Whitman and Alfred Lord Tennyson and a lot of even stranger people. Then on youth days I would periodically be the preacher, and that was enough to assure my extended family—and I think my mother too—that the call they heard was authentic, needing only the seasoning of time and the deepening of commitment, much seasoning and deepening—because I had some ways about me that they weren't quite sure were supposed to go with preaching in a Biblically-immersed community of saints.

But I hadn't stopped hearing the callings from other sources. In high school the teachers were the media, and I heard the call to high school teaching. Then one odd teacher told me I'd never pass the oral examination with such a wide space between my two front teeth. And high school teaching was put aside for a time.

Now, this thing with writing is part of the strangeness of the callings. I have not yet moved deeply enough into the chambers of the past to be certain about where and how it came. Perhaps the church community was the voice here too, encouraging my terrible poetry and acting as if my quarterly reports or my summaries and homilies on the Bible lessons were great documents (arousing, of course, certain contrary feelings among the younger members of my family-tribe at Victory Tabernacle Seventh Day Christian Church). That original voice is at least temporarily lost to me, but I know it existed, and if it was the community of believers, they likely did not know then that they had helped open me to one of the major tensions of my world of callings, a sometimes fierce stretching between writing and speaking, between writing and preaching, between scholarship and ministry in the midst of the people.

And by the time I got to college—somehow I think I always knew I had to go to college; and since there was absolutely no money for such a thing, I had to go to the only college I knew where you could at once attend without tuition and also have all the teachers and the loving tribe beam and say, "how wonderful, City College, that's a *hard* school to get into"—the loudest calling was towards writing, pressing me deeply into short story courses, journalism courses (finally majoring in History because there weren't enough writing courses), still experimenting with poetry, mostly devoted to working with the weekly campus newspaper, eventually becoming the inevitable FIRST NEGRO editor of that ancient institution of wisdom and scandal.

At City College, the calling towards writing meant another tension, pressed me towards a period of largely white friends and co-workers who vied with the ancestral community for my loyalties and my attention, led me into certain strange pathways which shut out voices I should have heard, led to great pain. But callings are strange things.

Some of the Tribe was likely worried when, after college, I went off to something else that wasn't really preaching, to graduate work in Journalism. (With all due respect to *their* worries, I was more worried about the Army then. That was a call I hoped to avoid for as long as possible.) Again the tensions of college were there, perhaps multiplied, as I was clearly being groomed for another FIRST NEGRO position. The serious and painful double voices were there, raising questions about the callings of the believers down the hill, through the park, in Harlem, and the callings which sometimes seemed so right and noble and GOOD FOR THE RACE) up at City College and over at Morningside Heights—and the worlds were deeply in tension. Callings will sometimes do that.

When I finally had to answer the call of the draft board, it was 1953. Knowing of no movement, lacking courage and desire to go the path of a C.O., which I did know a bit about—but didn't really hear that call, perhaps didn't want to—I went in. I wanted desperately to be sent to Germany or Japan or even Korea, any place outside of this country—for "education," not from alienation, yet. By then I thought I had filtered out the central call among the callings, and prepared for the next FIRST NEGRO experience, at some liberal newspaper, my preference, of course, being the New York *Times*. So, my post-Army movement seemed fairly well established as I went in, hearing all the raucous sounds of death and animality which substitute for life in the Army, but determining to be a good soldier, perhaps even an officer, getting overseas somewhere.

But in the strangeness that has surrounded so much of my life (coming, I know now, from deep sounding sources in the surrounding ancestral company of saints), I also decided, perhaps for the first time, to try to listen consciously, with anticipation, for the callings. I think I wanted to see if I would hear confirmations of the voices which had come through the believers or the teachers, seeking some release from the tension, suspecting perhaps that I might be pressed across new borders, following, listening. And in a place I never expected, under circumstances I would not have chosen, a brother spoke and asked me if I had ever thought of teaching; and for reasons far too complex and too far away to speak of now, I knew that I had heard the voice, the calling for that time.

(Strange about the Army. It never sent me anywhere, except Fort Dix, N.J. and Fort Benjamin Harrison, Indiana—partly because I knew how to type and play handball. Strange, too, that time of listening. I ended up rejecting all my inclinations towards the good soldier, became a C.O. in my heart. Strange, too: I had decided to engage in a very serious and sustained study of the Bible, partly for the listening, partly to prove to my girlfriend that she ought to be a Seventh Day Adventist like me. I did not know that in those long wrestlings with text and spirit I would be engaging in a major step on my journey beyond the borders of the loving family-tribe of believers at Victory Tabernacle [but like all tribal partings, of course, *never* being able to leave them].)

It was strange about the call. I still had the words of the odd high school teacher in my mind, and decided that if I were going to teach it might be better to try college, where I assumed that spaces between teeth didn't count. But I knew nothing about graduate schools, and finally, when pressed to choose among the ones where I had been accepted, opened myself with fear and trembling to the voice of the tribe/community/church, and went to Chicago—two weeks after discharge from the Army—where I could be of assistance as interim, part-time pastor of a little mission congregation that Victory Tabernacle sponsored there. That made the graduate school acceptable, worldly as they knew it was. Now, I would be anchored in an extension of the tribe; so they thought the calls and prayers had finally drawn me out of the strange and various paths I had explored.

How do you explain it? Callings are strange things. In Chicago, for the first time—after having grown up in Harlem and the Bronx—strangely it was in Chicago that I finally heard and saw the Black urban condition in America. On the Southside, I heard its singing and its screams, saw its determination and its terror, sensed its freedom and its captivity. And while there was much I did not then understand about such calls, I knew this was calling me.

One day I shall try to understand and speak more fully of the painful calling which took me away from the little mission congregation—and ultimately away from my immediate (but not my ultimate) relationship to the tribe of my childhood and my youth. That calling is not fully clear to me yet, and even if it were, it is not yet time to speak of it. This much can be said: the move to an interracial congregation as a lay pastor of a team ministry seemed to allow me to hold the tension of Blackness and whiteness (it was, of course, a time when such things seemed most urgent), the tension of teaching and preaching, of study and ministry. But those are only superficial statements, and should be received as such for now.

Nor is it yet time to speak fully of the ultimately transforming call that led to marriage, a call far different than any I had known, a call I was in too many ways unprepared to understand in all the richness of its meanings and its summons. But I know it is a calling, mine.

Then, before graduate work had ended, the call of the Southern Freedom Movement became overwhelming, pressing aside almost every other voice. There was no escaping it. It possessed me during my first, exploring journey into the South, (grasped me there sitting on Martin King's bed in Montgomery where he rested recovering from his stabbing). It came to Chicago in the body of the students and found me. While sit-ins and freedom-rides were still sweeping across the South, we left Chicago and went South, hearing, following a call.

We shall understand it better by and by, and also speak more clearly of it, that calling. Now let it suffice to say that it was then that all the fiercely gripping, special callings of the South began, calls of the Movement, of Southwest Georgia (home of my wife's parents, repository of so many memories of hope and fear), of all the stretching land upon which my people walked, and worked, and ran, and stood, and died. Then it began, all the callings of Birmingham and Tuskegee, of Montgomery and Mobile, of Jackson and Meridian, of Gulfport and Greenwood, of New Orleans and Charleston, of Hickory and Atlanta, of Ella Baker and Amzie Moore, of Ralph Abernathy and Bill Shields, of Bob Moses Parris and Annelle Ponder, of Jim and Diane, of Septima Clark and Slater King, of Clarence Jordan and Staughton Lynd—this was the beginning of new callings.

And when, after four years that encompassed a generation of struggle, when the Movement had passed its height, it was possible to hear strange callings through personal tragedy, and there were endings and beginnings again. Then finally the finishing of graduate work and the beginning of teaching—still with a space between the front two teeth.

There the latest callings began. From somewhere—

had Buddha visited?—there was an urgent aching to understand the meaning of Vietnam, and on the 20th anniversary of Hiroshima, that need plunged me past the superficial surfaces of my knowing, brought me in touch with the meaning of that brutal tale, that heroic defense of life, and provided new impetus for my continuing movement away from this America, towards a radically transformed society.

Teaching, spaces and all. There the latest callings began. Teaching history I was called to understand how little I knew of history. Teaching Black students, I learned how little this Black student, this FIRST NEGRO, had been taught, especially about the truth of his own long pilgrimage, about his people's struggles against the powers of death, about their determined movement towards new life. And when I knew that, I began—as in the Army, only a different army now—to listen again, hearing some things that I had let slip by in the days of the Tribe, understanding things I had only seen in the Movement. I began to hear voices more loudly than ever before, and they will not be silent, for they are me.

I hear all the varied sounds of my homeland, all its human sounds, all its animals, its spirit-filled rivers and lakes, its waterfalls, its mountains, its grass and trees playing with the wind. I hear them all.

I hear all the screaming of my homeland, all the mournful pacing down to the slave baracoons, all the piercing, dying shouts, all the parting wailing sounds. I hear children, crying children, I hear men, I hear women, calling, now desiring only to be remembered, and vindicated. I hear them between the decks of the ships called *Jesus* and *St. John,* and *Liberty,* and *Justice.* I hear their whispers and then their bursting yells as they come on decks prepared to die, and, if necessary, to kill for their freedom. I hear them calling, falling on the decks, thrown, often leaping to their ending —but not ending—in the waters. I hear them singing as they go under the waves—free.

I hear my people. I hear them calling from Virginia to San Francisco, I hear their songs and their cries and their defiant shouts and their long silences through all the horrors called slavery. I hear them lost in the wilderness, I hear them moving, seeking the North Star, determined to make their way to freedom.

I hear them in preaching and praying, holding one another through hunger and parting, through torture and sickness, through childbirth and dying, I hear them calling.

I hear my people, lurching, flooding towards freedom during the Civil War, seizing their own liberty. I hear them fighting and falling, rising and hoping again. I hear them in all the halcyon hopeful first days of Reconstruction, in all the bloody years that followed, when hope was crushed by the force of white arms and the power of white betrayals.

I hear them, mourning, weeping, wailing, prostrate around the thousands of trees where brothers and sisters were hung and burned and mutilated beyond recognition by a savage people. I hear them vowing never to give in, never to turn back, to endure, to resist, to live, to go on. I hear their calling.

I hear them coming North, I hear them in the armies, I hear them in the mills, I hear them in the railroads, I hear them in the fires, I hear them in the waters, I hear Nat Turner and David Walker, I hear Douglass and Delaney, I hear Harriet and Sojourner, I hear Ida B. Wells and Bishop Turner, I hear Garvey and DuBois, I hear Bessie Smith. I hear them calling.

I hear them in depression, picking their way through garbage piles, sharing even that with one another. I hear them calling for Robeson, for Father, for Daddy, for Adam, for Solidarity, for help.

I hear them in war, dying for a land that will not protect them. I hear them coming beyond war to struggle for truth. I hear them in court. I hear them in the streets. I hear ladies walking in Montgomery. I hear Martin preaching in the churches, hear his footsteps on the road. I hear old folks singing in churches, standing before dogs. I hear students risking their lives, freezing in jail, singing while hungry, laughing when afraid, not being overcome. I hear them calling.

I hear my people marching, refusing to stop, refusing to be quiet, refusing to be satisfied, refusing to die.

I hear Malcolm, I hear Stokely, I hear Rap and Feather, I hear Ruby and Jim. I hear Jonathan. I hear Angela. I hear Attica. I hear dying Panthers and preachers. I hear living men and women. I hear them. I hear voices, and I know what it means.

Callings are a strange thing. I know what it means: I am a witness, in spite of myself, beyond myself, and their voices must be heard.

I am a witness, (teacher, preacher, ranter, raver, dissident, resistant, radical, revolutionary, silent carrier) witness to their truth and power, pressed forward by the force of their being, by the integrity of their struggle, by the silent roaring of their voices. No turning back.

I know what it means: I am historian—now recognizing all the long ago callings—summoned to tell their story, for them, for myself, for our children. They shall not be forgotten.

It means I am now of them, deep calling unto deep. Their voice has entered so profoundly into me that I am flesh of their flesh, bone of their bone, song of their song, pain of their pain, hope of their hope. Forever lost to scholarly "objectivity," forever seared by the passion of their fiery movement, unwilling and unable to be detached from their struggle. Bound by cords of life and death and love—and intimations of the morning. Privileged, permitted, summoned to join them, their struggle is mine, and I am called forward into tomorrow, searching for the way to carry the struggle, to break the bonds, to build the new land of their hopes.

(Callings are strange things. They find you in the midst of your own family.)

I hear my mother, sighing, scrubbing all the floors in all the white homes, bearing with love and pain and anxious prayer the burden that I was/am. (I would like to hear my father, and one day I suspect I shall.) I know it means I am still son, hope, strength, promise for tomorrow, beyond all the pain and death.

I hear voices—of my children, Rachel Sojourner and Jonathan DuBois. I believe that ancient rivers of our people flow in them. I hear their voices, and I know what it means. It means I am called to be father, rock and strength, encourager for the struggles of tomorrow, baptizer in the rivers of their past.

I hear a voice, of my wife, Rosemarie. I know what it means. I am to be husband and man, strength and solace, lover and companion in the way, resting place and summons to joy in the morning.

Callings are strange things. I think I have heard many voices in many times and places, but it may be that I have heard only One.

The Monastic Calling

Matthew Kelty

Father Kelty is a member of the Order of Cistercians of the Strict Observance, called Trappist. Recently at the Monastery of the Holy Mother of God, Oxford, North Carolina, he is presently stationed in Papua, New Guinea.

The following reflections on the monastic scene (of the Cistercian variety) were written by way of offering some introductory matter for those expressing interest in the monks' way of life, a desire to look into it, perhaps join. With contemporary interest in communal living, it was thought that the monastic approach might be of interest: monks have been living in community a long time. The Cistercians have been at it since 1098, and they are late-comers.

After living in a large monastery, Gethsemani, Kentucky, for a dozen years, I was sent to this experimental community in North Carolina. There is considerable wonder these days whether or not the small monastery may not also be a valid form, if only an alternate one. Small in every sense: a small "plant," a few members, and also a modest or simple style of life in all areas. We do not plan on having more than six and as yet have not had that many monks: the number has been up and down over the past two years. While larger monasteries have a rather elaborate liturgy, and admittedly one of great beauty and dignity, here we simply read the psalms, all of them in a course of a week, spreading them out over three sessions each day, one at three in the morning (the night is a time for love), one at dawn, one at sunset. With the psalms we add a long continued reading from the Old Testament, the Gospels, and the rest of the New Testament. We close with the Our Father and Hail Mary. We have the Eucharist after the morning session at dawn. Mornings are given to work, chores and household duties and weaving, our source of income. Weaving has turned out a happy choice, appropriate to the area (yarn is not hard to find), perfectly adapted to our kind of life, and a very good craft, creative and rewarding, even for beginners. The noon meal is our one common meal and we talk at it, not the usual monastic custom. It serves

as our noon "liturgy" and companion to the morning
Eucharist. Afternoons we are free for reading or prayer
or work if we choose, so long as it be quiet. And we
leave one another be during those hours.

There are obvious advantages to such a style of
life: there is plenty of quiet and seclusion, loneliness:
a good setting for prayer. We are fortunate in having
a good library, and the area is attractive, a wooded
tract off the highway, seven miles from town. The people are friendly and yet do not overwhelm us, respect-
ing what we are trying to do.

The buildings include an attractive chapel, a main
building with library, kitchen and refectory, washroom,
and rooms for guests. There are five cabins or cells for
the individual monks, scattered around the place, and
we use a mobile home for the weaving shop. Out back
is a good work shop, the chicken coop, the tobacco
patch (this is Carolina); we do not work the tobacco
since we know nothing about it. A neighbor does it.
It would not be fair to omit the cat and the dog since
they are very much part of the place.

Two years is too short a time to justify much pre-
diction, but at least we are still here, still with it, and
happy with it. It is hard to think of places of this sort
managing without relation to some larger monastery,
but there does seem good reason to think that as an
alternate style of monastic life, it is worth experimenting
with. The larger the place, the more likely it will take
on institutional aspects, a feature not too much in demand these days. No one would be so bold as to think
the smaller place better, but it is clear to me that they
do offer genuine experience of what the monk is after.

Things like turtle doves and peacocks and guinea
hens and goats add a good touch. We have a handsome

sundial, a good garden, and while we wear the habit (the cowl) only in chapel, the place has a definite monastic tone and is a lovely spot.

Life itself is mystery. It would follow that major aspects of life are involved with mystery. Birth and death, marriage and child-birth—these are mighty deep. It is to say nothing original, then, to say that a calling to the monastic life is a mysterious thing.

Response to mystery can be positive, however. While silent wonder is a most appropriate posture, the Christian realizes that it is in prayer that man best meets the unknown and the unfathomable. This is, in fact, the only way to encounter God and those times we come closest to God acting in our lives.

A calling to the monastic life is a call first of all to prayer. Serious, deep, abiding prayer. Prayer is communication, the relation of Lover to loved one. It is not so much a matter of words as of attitudes, a disposition of the heart and a frame of mind.

A man who is beginning to wonder whether or not he should become a monk is a wise man if he makes the wonder a form of prayer. He is touching something very awesome, indeed, very terrible. He may get burned. In any case, the whole business is something he will never forget as long as he lives.

Over a period of years I talked with many hundreds of men interested in one way or another in becoming monks. I never entered such dialogues light-heartedly and never left them without a feeling of having been in some kind of sanctuary. The boxes were of all sizes and shapes and forms: those who brought them were anxious to open them and show me the contents. I never lifted the lid without reverence. Prayer was the only climate for such doings.

COMMUNITY

A monk is a member of a community. Though the calling is basically solitary (*monos* means alone), it is normally acted out in a community, in a monastery. When one thinks of monks one thinks of monasteries.

One joins such a community in the expectation that here one will find like-minded brethren in search of a common goal. It is common goals that gather men: selling insurance, climbing mountains, playing chess. The "search for God" is what monks have in common. More than that, a search for God within a certain frame of reference, within a certain tradition.

A Benedictine follows the rule handed down by Saint Benedict and his followers. There are many varieties of Benedictines, among them being Cistercians. There are even varieties of Cistercians, and, for all that, one Cistercian monastery will differ from another. Yet a Cistercian is a recognizable Benedictine and every Cistercian monastery will have something in common with every house in the Order.

The Order, the Rule, the monastery is there to provide the means by which one follows a calling to the love and service of God. Monks do not keep monasteries going, and monasteries the Order. It is the other way around.

But it is important to see the service that monasteries and orders provide. They have a tradition, a history, a patrimony. When they are in touch with this tradition, are faithful to it, and have profound understanding of it, we have the ideal situation. Every monastery tries to keep in touch with its basic spirit and exemplify it in the contemporary scene.

It is this sense of history which gives great strength to a monastic group. Any man anywhere, any group of men anywhere, could become monks. But you may be sure they would endeavor very soon to get in touch with a tradition, either through living monks or through texts, in order to pick up the thread of continuity.

There is nothing unusual in this: doctors are in a sense in living touch with the whole past medical profession. But it is important to grasp its significance. It is a bit more than merely carrying on an old tradition. Monks are not museum keepers or museum pieces. But monks do have a sense of history. And it is this which gives their lives depth and scope. A people without history is a people in danger, for they have lost touch with their roots.

It is through his community that the monk is in touch with the whole monastic charism and its discipline. By means of the community he comes to know the gift of God and how to respond to it. A monastery is often compared to the Church for the reason that as one is in union with Christ through the Church, so one by his community works out his relationship to his calling from God in a context of human history.

SERVICE

It is in community that one learns a discipline of service. And it is this discipline in turn which opens one to the workings of God in the spirit. For a group of men to live together in harmony and peace there must be sacrifice and generosity. The good of the brethren and the interests of others must often take precedence over one's own desires. Selfless service of others is a good school of love.

And yet it is love of a particular sort. It is different from familial love, since a monastery is not strictly speaking a family. The relation of husband and wife, parents and children is not there. We speak of the "monastic family," but only in a loose sense of the word. It would be fatal to look for the monastic community to supply what one would normally have in a family.

It is more than fraternal love, since a monastery is not just a fraternity. One does speak more correctly of the monks having brotherly love for one another, yet even this must be understood correctly. They are a lot more than "buddies." More than comrades. More even than brothers in the flesh. Their love for one another is primarily in Christ. It is because they love Christ that they love one another.

The ideal of monastic love is noble and, given an experience of human nature in depth, a demanding discipline. It takes time and effort and grace to bring it about, but a community of men with genuine love for one another in Christ is a great joy. It is a profound force in the world, able to move mountains. It will not always be obvious, even to those who share in it. This kind of love is deeper than smiles and camaraderie, a certain effusive sentiment. It is the kind of love that makes death for one's brother easy and understandable and common.

Thus, among other things, monks wash each other's clothes and do the dishes, cook the food and clean the toilets; they type letters and milk cows, wash sinks and make cheese, bake cake and bread, and get dinner ready. They work, as all men work for a living, and endeavor to work literally for love of God and one another.

And it is this discipline of service which opens the heart and makes a man available to the Lord God who would woo his heart if He could get close enough. It is service that lets God in because self has been driven out.

PRAYER

The monk is called to a life of prayer. The traditional prayer of the monk is the Book of Psalms and hence it has become traditional also to think of the monk as one who loves to pray these Psalms. This is still true. The Psalter is the monk's prayer book. The saying or the chanting of Psalms is still basic to the monk's life. Here too there have been various changes in the course of history as to manners and methods in the praying of the Psalter. At times the monks have said a great many Psalms in a day, sometimes in rather elaborate forms.

In connecting psalmody and monk we bring together two important elements: that a monk is a man of prayer and that the monk is a man of the Psalter.

The monk is a man of prayer and the monastery is there to help him achieve this. To pray means to make love to God, to be in touch with God, in communion with Him. This could mean long hours in church, many hours with divine service: it need not. What it does mean and what is basic is that the monk lives in a setting, an atmosphere, a world of prayer. He is a man to whom prayer is his life, his love. In a sense he is always at prayer. This prayer may at times be formal and explicit: Holy Mass, for example. At other times, quiet and informal. But it is more or less always there somehow or other, one way or other. It is as a man with a good wife: she is in a sense never out of his mind and heart, never far from him.

The Psalter is the monk's book because the monk is a man in touch with the whole world. From his own heart he knows what life is and what man is. The Psalter is a man's book of prayer. It is deep and mysterious. It plumbs to man's depths and ascends to his highest peaks. Here is man at his worst and at his best. Here are thoughts best not mentioned and desires best left lie. Here is man as he is, calling on the Redeemer and the Savior. The monk loves the Psalter because it covers the familiar ground of his own heart. In it he reads his own mind and says what his lips hardly would otherwise dare form. The Psalter is not a pretty book, but it is a real one. It is in touch with reality.

That is why the test of the monk has always been the Psalter. Saint Benedict was always anxious to know whether the monk loved the Psalms or not. He was shrewd, for it is a good test. If a monk can take up the Psalter and read it out of his own heart and make it his own, then he knows what it's all about. He is with it. Until then he is just skimming along.

In which case, just let him stay with it. Let him taste hours of darkness. Let him know silence. Let him do humble services to his brethren. Let him go a little hungry. Let him taste his own poverty. And then, with the help of God and His Holy Mother, the thing will open up for him. A bit at a time. He will feel something between his teeth. And the Psalter will come to life.

POVERTY

People in an affluent society are always charmed with the "simple life," a religious poverty, practiced by others. It makes them feel better, less guilty. If they could hire a group of holy women to live an edifying poverty for their sakes, they would do so.

That is one approach. There are many others.

For a group of men to pool their resources and live in community of ownership makes a lot of sense and by some is understood to be a form of "poverty."

It is also a recognized form of "poverty" to live in a simple style of life synonymous with plain living.

To live in dependence on a superior and without jurisdiction over one's material resources is also one expression of "poverty."

The monk's "poverty" is probably a bit of all these. Though sometimes a monk may live in a rather primitive setting with a style of monastic buildings which is clearly redolent of the original Citeaux, it is even more likely that he will live in a rather handsome complex. But even here he may find the overall impression rather severely simple and, to some minds, cold and austere. The point of buildings is that they serve the monk, that they help him do what he came to the monastery to do. There is no question that men are influenced by their environment, and the monk by his. It is possible to build such an environment as to serve the monk well, and this is something monks continue to try to do. They sometimes succeed. Sometimes there is a sort of compromise in which the result is over or under the mark.

The sum of all this is read in the monk's heart, for there is the true field of action for poverty. The monk's style of life may be awesome in its rigor, it may be dangerously close to the style of the well-heeled: he can get as used to one as to the other and live interiorly without reference to either. Most monks, however, need something going outside to keep the inner fire burning.

Yet it remains true: it is the inner fire that matters. Without that nothing has much meaning. External poverty can become an obsession and a worse problem than wealth. And a wealthy monastery often wishes it weren't. Even so, one forgets that it is not the same thing to share a lot of common wealth and to own it personally; all groups have problems getting members to take good care of equipment and machinery, tools and supplies, for the obvious reason that it is one thing to own something and quite another to have the use of it.

The monastic program of silence and solitude, of work and service, of worship and obedience of community life will bring the monk to such an experience of inner desolation and destitution as to make everything else pale. In such a setting a man may learn a little about humility, may shed some of his arrogance and come down to size; may taste of despair and his own futile existence, may develop a sense of trust in Providence and a hope in salvation through Christ the Lord. He may, in short, come to be a poor man. If he is willing to walk that road with the Lord, he will find a real kingdom, the one promised the poor.

OBEDIENCE

If a man can learn the secret of obedience he will be well on his way to the secret of the monastic life. It is quite true to say that there is risk in many aspects of the monastic life: there are dangers in silence and solitude; those not prepared for it and not equal to it may find the monastic life may bring them to the shores of breakdown. This does not mean that monastic life is sick: it means that there are people to whom an inner experience is better left be. There is no need to fear any of this. If one is candid with those who interview when one enters, speaks freely with his abbot or director, all will be well.

There is however a certain risk involved in obedience that must be taken and is essential to the monastic life. One must learn somehow to take one's life in one's hands and place it in the hands of another. This sounds easy. It isn't. It is very difficult. There are one million ways to do it and slip out of it. Until you have tried to do it you have no business discussing it. It may happen many times, but it is certain to happen at least once that one's whole life depends on a moment's willingness to lay it on the line. This happens to most people. To anyone willing to look closely there may come a moment in one's life which is in every sense of the word a moment of destiny, a moment to which one can, in later years, look back and realize that everything was leading to that point, and everything flows thence from it. There is no way of knowing when such a moment may come; indeed, one may not even recognize it until long after. But one thing is certain: you will muff it unless you have learned how to lay it on the line. And the secret in that art is simple: you have to risk all to gain all. And though there is a lot of talk about risk theology, you will find that there is not too much of it practiced.

The whole point and purpose of this obedience is to put one in a proper relationship to God. There cannot possibly be any dialogue between God and man unless there is an openness, a willingness to listen on the part of man. This is not to be assumed as present. Further, there is necessary for God's action on the human soul such a willingness to be at His disposal, almost a mere putty in His hands, that unless a man be willing to learn it by the hard discipline of obedience may not be learned at all. In that case one simply does not achieve the growth he was called to, for it must be understood that the mature life, the holy life, is one in which one lives at one's peak level, for all one is worth. Achievement is the fruit of discipline and discipline is not easily come by. It is simply naive to assume that one can achieve anything in terms of a relationship to God unless one is quite willing at a moment's notice to lay one's life down for Him. After all, being true to one's own truth is also a matter of listening and responding, and it is one's own truth one responds to in listening to God. If the obedient man will speak of victory, it is also the obedient man who is master of his own destiny.

There is no aspect of monastic life more difficult than this, none more misunderstood, and for all that, misused. Be that as it may, it remains the key and was much stressed by Saint Benedict and by all monastic teachers.

FASTING

Fasting is no longer fashionable in most quarters today. There are, to be sure, vast areas of our own land and of the world where few get enough to eat, but the voluntary denial of food to one's self for spiritual reasons is not very common. There is a considerable amount of vanity fasting or weight-watching, but that is not fasting.

Notwithstanding the trends of the age, monks still fast. They do not eat meat at all, and the mortification of the appetite by abstemious eating at certain seasons or at certain times is still recognized as a sound practice in the ascetic life.

Western man has not done too well in the development of techniques in prayer and contemplation; it would follow that he has not properly understood the role of fasting. With the growing awareness of the great value of many practices of the Orient in forms and methods of prayer, we may be sure that fasting will come into its own once again.

The curbing of the appetites, the calming of the passions, the control of one's impulses and urges, drives, is basic to the monastic life and a hope to move in the depth of one's prayer without growth in self-control is naive in the extreme. Not to kill human capacities, not to succumb to them, but to perfect them: to make an art of life.

For the sake of the beginner, however, let us say that in this matter environment can be of great help. A consumer-oriented social setting is not the best preparation for a life of denial. A monastic environment is perhaps a little better. In a world free of frantic stimulation of the sexual and consumer-appetites it is rather much easier to get a better hold of one's self and learn the beauty of being master of one's flesh and one's stomach.

Fasting cools one's heat, slows one down, softens the harshness of one's self-assertion, makes one more gentle and calm. It does these things when done well.

If fasting is simply made an act of prowess and a bit of vulgar display, nothing will come of it.

Dependent characters often find fasting very difficult and entertain exaggerated notions of their need for nourishment. A society almost infantile in its need for something to drink, something to chew on, something to taste, to suck, to inhale is scarcely one to encourage self-sufficiency and independence, but in a monastery one will find the climate somewhat healthier.

In this matter practically all is left to one's own discretion and the guidance of one's spiritual father, since former detailed rulings imposed on all no longer are the order of the day. Now matters can be adjusted to the personal needs of each.

ON JESUS

The whole thing revolves around Christ and love for Him, the Lord and the Savior. Christ is not just your older Brother, though He is that too if you like. But more than that, He is God and Man, Redeemer, Savior. He is most of all Perfect Man, Whole Man, Man entire and intact,
Man beautiful and holy, Man complete and fulfilled.
He is poet and mystic,
He is dreamer and savant,
He is leader and teacher. He lived, He taught, He suffered, He died and
He rose from the dead and ascended into the Heaven to which He leads us and calls us.
He would have us follow Him, in living and in dying, in rising and ascending with Him.
He is part of all human life and all human history and would have us join Him in that experience of organic and spiritual unity.

He is wed to the whole human family as His bride and
   unless you are willing to take the whole human
   family to your own heart, He will have no part
   of you.

He calls on men to suffer and to die with Him and for
   Him for His own; you are called to that also.

His Church is His continued presence on earth: the
   Church is His spouse intimate and close, chosen,
   elected, ravished by His love for her and through
   her for all of man.

Unless you have a passionate love for Holy Church,
   bride of Christ, it would be better not to come
   close.

He is present in His church in her teaching and her holy
   life, which is His life flowing through her and into
   the whole world.

The church is a great mystery, but a great love first
   of all.

The monk is called to grow in love for her,

for Christ's life in her,

through her.

Pope and Bishop and Priest are more than just people
   to the monk, more than just churchmen.

And his life in the church is sustained by an eating of
   the Body of the Lord and the drinking of His
   Holy Blood.

For that Lord he would gladly die, as for Him he gladly
   and joyously lives.

Christ is the beginning of the monk's day, and its end.

Christ is the point of the monastic life, its core and purpose.

Without Him it is just pious exercise.

With Him it is a love affair without parallel this side of
   eternity.

THE ABBOT

   The role of the abbot in the monastery and in the
monk's life is at once pivotal and tender. It is quite true

to say that the life of the monks revolves around the abbot: in a sense he sets the tone of the place and gives it the quality and character it has. On the other hand, there is nothing automatic about it. We deal with something very fragile and delicate. When it works it is wonderful; but even when it doesn't, when the abbot or the monks or both are not quite what they should be, it still has something sacramental about it: a medium of grace and light notwithstanding human foible. This is said not so much to canonize incompetence and inadequacy—as if there were something divine about bungling—but simply to encourage: human situations are generally less than ideal. There is a kind of refuge in perfectionism which serves as solace for aggressive characters which will never come up to the basic issue: a matter of faith.

The monk reaches his abbot in faith or he does not reach him at all. In a sense he acts out the ancient quest for the spiritual father and submits himself to his regimen in order to become a free man. His confidence in the father helps him make the plunge, but no matter how worthy the spiritual guide, it is the disciple who must in the end make the jump: inadequacy in the father will never make up for want of courage in the son. There are monks who get nowhere and blame their abbot. It is not always quite so pat.

The abbot, when he dances well, is at once a leader and a follower. He is under oath to maintain the rule and yet he is also one who deals with human persons. The more truly he listens to God, which is to say the holier he is, the more surely will he listen to men, since God is everywhere. A true abbot does not follow his flock wherever they would go, nor does he drive them after his own designs. He does something of both.

He is like Christ and His church, like a Bishop and his diocese, a pastor and his parish, a husband and his wife. A man who does not listen to his wife misses the secret. On the other hand, you cannot dance with anyone who will never lead.

The monk sees Christ in his abbot, not as an act of the imagination, but as an expression of faith in something deeper than skin. In this relationshp he grows in love and responds to the action of God in his own history.

Abbots fail. So do monks. And monasteries. Not to say marriages. But if you want something guaranteed not to fail, are you able to love? Failures, after all, are part of the success. And in any case we are not always sure which is which.

There is no question, that in the monk's role in relation to his abbot we touch on one of the most profound aspects of the monastic life. That being so, it is best to approach it in faith first of all. That is the only realistic approach. Anything short of that is simply not in touch with the total picture.

Anyone thinking about the monastic life might well dwell with these thoughts awhile. It is one thing to view the ship from the dock and dream of far-away places; It is quite another to be on board, and in every kind of weather.

SILENCE

Perhaps one of the things that is envied in the monk's life is his silence. In a world becoming daily more noisy, the idea of a place of quiet, of a life in which there are areas of silence becomes very attractive.

Much of the contemporary racket is deliberate, most of it is not necessary. Once the law gets on the side of the citizenry, it ought to be possible to bring some of these violators of our rights to heel: these madmen who zoom over our heads with an ear-splitting roar, for example. There ought to be a very special corner in the next life where those who afflicted us with noise in this life could atone for what they did. Indeed, I am sure there is.

Silence is a privilege to which all are entitled and of which most are robbed in this barbaric age. The monk is not a freak for loving silence; he is simply normal and human.

The average monastery is not nearly as quiet as it should be, since the monks come from a noisy world and think noise a quality of all genuine life. Only slowly do they learn the beauty and meaning of quiet. Machinery is noisy and monks are from a machine age and seem to need a lot of it.

Despite these drawbacks, silence is a real part of monastic life. It is perhaps the greatest single factor in spiritual growth. Without it nothing can happen.

It is not a matter of taciturnity. Men who do not easily and happily communicate with their fellowmen do not make good monks. A lack of sensitivity to others is no sign of a Trappist vocation. On the other hand, the monk must gradually acquire a feeling for silence. Unless the monks in the monastery are aware of the point of quiet, they will not build a quiet house. And a quiet house is the basic background.

One reason monks rise early to pray is the quiet of the night. Darkness is a kind of visual quiet and monks love it. The hours before dawn are sacred.

Silence need not make monks a weird crew, though

this sometimes happens when common sense is abandoned. Monks in former times went to great lengths to "keep silence." Their efforts strike modern man as somewhat theatrical and showy. But unless a man can see the point of silence he might just as well not bother coming to the monastery. It is inevitable that the whole thing will never mean anything to him. He has to have a feeling for this kind of thing.

Simply has to.

SECLUSION

Most people today take a dim view of the monk's desire for seclusion. They see it as "flight" and do not appreciate the monk for "fleeing." Perhaps flight is not the best word.

Certainly the monk does not escape anything. Nor does he desire to.

Pressed to explain, the monk might perhaps turn the thing around and say that it was precisely because he was tired of running that he became a monk. Taken from one point of view, who is more "in flight" than the "man of the world"? When one talks of escape, one might more likely look elsewhere than a monastery if he wants to see it in action.

People in flight had best not come to monasteries. And those who desire to escape had best look down another road. This is no place for the timid and the skittish. Those who fear their own depths and the deep of night had better find something to occupy them or to divert them.

There is nothing wrong with that. God has not

called everyone to the inner experience. Not all are equal to it. Some shy away from their own depths with very good reason. Solitude is not everyone's dish, nor the lonely life.

But it is a bit unfair to call those who embark upon it men in flight. The monk is a man of his time and when he goes into the desert, he takes his world with him. Every man's heart is a little universe and to understand one's time one need only read one's own heart, honestly and truly.

The monk sees quiet and peace and seclusion not to get away from "the world," but to get closer to it. Not to shut out the voice of man, but to listen to it. Not to flee the time's ills, but to heal them.

This is the center of the monk's whole life. The purpose of the monastery is to provide a setting in which this inner business can go on. The monastic community can be a lot of things and is many things to many people, but it is this inner activity that is the very heart. Without this it is simply not a monastery, and with it, the place is justified.

The style of monastic seclusion varies from age to age. As in other areas, there are styles here too. Architecture, vesture, daily schedules, diet, means of income —all these change from time to time. And so do the forms of seclusion. At one time high walls and big gates were the thing. At another an absolute interdict on newspapers and magazines. At another visits at the monastery or out of it. There are many varieties of religious experience in terms of monastic seclusion. But if it is a monastery that makes any pretense at contemplative life there will be some sort of guarantee that the monks have all the experience of silence and solitude that they want and need. Without this the vine withers and dies and the place becomes a harmless addition to the landscape.

CELIBACY

The monk is a celibate. It is at least theoretically possible to speak of a married clergy. It is not possible to speak of a married monk. A married man might become a monk, and a monk might become a married man, but a monk is not married. He is celibate. He is virginal.

Christ was a virgin. The monk follows Him in this. Christ took to wife the people of Israel; His spouse is the Church. The monk does as much also, taking to wife the monastery as the miniature church. For this church, model of the Church itself, and image of the whole world, the monk gives himself to God and serves this people for love.

But it is basically an inner reality. Man is two-dimensional and spends his life bringing about a basic harmony and eventual unity of the forces within him. Most people do this through marriage. In the kingdom of heaven there will be no marriage and giving in marriage because there we will have attained basic wholeness. There we will be as the angels, not in having no bodies, but in having fulness of being.

The monk lives the angelic life on earth, not through having no body, or worse, pretending he had none, but seeking to achieve the inner unity by the wholeness of his life.

This is no small goal. If human marriage does not always come off as well as was hoped for, it can be assumed that the virginal life is not without its hazards.

But some hazards are necessary and worth taking. Those who respond to a call to virginity are taking a risk and venturing on a difficult road. They might as well face that. Let him who can take it, take it.

There have always been monks where there has been a developed culture, and there have always been virgins and celibates. This is as old as human nature. Priests and poets and artists and celibates are part of the human scene, always have been and always will be.

There have always been men and women who have been aware of a call to wholeness by way of the inner experience. There are such today too. Monks are men of this group. There are people who think of the celibate as loveless. This is a horrible thought. Celibacy is precisely a way of love. It is love not through the physical body and sexual communion, but on the mystical and spiritual plane. It is not a matter of a better love: it is love on a different level. It is love in a different mode. Love of another kind. Married people are also capable of this sort of love—as indeed all men and women are. But the monk, the celibate, makes a total plunge into this manner of love and by means of it seeks in the grace of God to reach deep into the mystery of love for God and man.

Not everyone appreciates this or desires it. That is not the point. The monk feels called to it. In the case of the monk it has nothing to do with contempt for woman: contempt for woman is no sign of a call to virginity. Certainly not to consecrated virginity. Nor is homosexual love involved, since it is sexual.

In some regions of the earth and in some religions, men enter into a monastic form of life after having been married and having raised a family. There is much to be said for this, and it points out that in addition to married love, there is another and different kind of love which is expressed in the celibate state. In this instance, the experience of married love would be a benefit in growth in divine love. On the other hand, there have always been men who in early years have chosen the celibate way and have lived it throughout their lives.

This is not an easy road nor a light discipline, but it is of profound beauty and meaning, and opens up riches of spiritual experience for the good of man and for the glory of God.

The monastery seeks to provide such a setting as will make this celibate life a fruitful one and with a balanced life of prayer, work, and reading help the monk achieve a maturity in love which grace led him to.

SOLITUDE

Monks are lonely men. This does not make them particularly different, since most men are lonely. It is what they do with their loneliness that makes them somewhat different.

One good reason for community is to teach the monk how to live with loneliness. There are men who are "loners" by nature or by instinct. They would not necessarily make good monks, in fact it is not likely that they would. The monk usually is very social and likes people. But he has a dimension which is open to solitude. All men have this dimension, but not all are interested in it or want to cultivate it. Monks are much interested in the solitary aspects of life because it is here that one best meets God.

We come into the world alone and we leave it alone, no matter how many attend us. Man has an infinite loneliness, a loneliness without measure. On this seashore the monk often walks and ponders. Under this lonely sky he often stands. At such times he does nothing, for there is nothing you can do. But he lets it happen to him. He lets it sink in.

His greatest help in learning this art is community. It is the experience of deep love that makes it possible for one to accept the large experience of solitude. And the deeper the experience of love, the more intense the entry into the depths of one's being.

A community in which genuine love flourishes will also be a community in which there is a great love for solitude, for the reason that one leads to the other. It is the experience of genuine love that gives one the courage to stand alone before God.

Solitude is an environment of love and only those who have known love can enter upon it fruitfully. There are many lonely people, but not all of them are in love. It is the monk's desire to enter into the mystery of love in its ultimate expression, deep in his own heart. Community life prepares him for this.

TO BE DISCOURAGED

Some kinds of people are much drawn to monasteries and must be warned that such a life is not good for them and may even do them much harm. Normally such characters will be noted before they enter, but a great deal of anguish can be spared them if they do not even move that far along the road toward something that is not meant for them.

People with emotional hangups of serious dimensions — enough to require hospitalization or long therapy with psychiatrists—ought to stay clear of monasteries no matter how strongly they feel that God is calling them to enter one.

Let us put it plainly: monastic life is no picnic. Day by day there is really nothing very difficult about it, but put a number of days in a row, one after another, and certain types are apt to climb the walls. Some people cannot stand silence, seclusion, monotony, quiet, a lack of excitement and diversion. Neurotic, psychotic types surely not.

If you do not like people, the monastery is no place to go. If you hate the world, this is no place to come. If you get moody and depressed, this will crush you for sure.

To ask for healthy young men from a culture as sick as ours is to ask a great deal. But there must be a certain amount of good sense, of courage, and of enthusiasm. There will have to be a love for life and a desire to truly live.

Narrowing it down to what makes the contemplative calling we might add: a sense of wonder.

And a certain intuitive grasp that there is something else besides action. That while action is good enough and absolutely necessary, there is another side to the coin: there is something to be said for musing, for pondering, for mulling.

There ought to be a desire to go to some place where men pray, yes; where they work, yes; where they read good books, yes . . . but in addition to that, where they do nothing. Where the pause that refreshes is not a drink . . . a place for men who love the night, and know the moon, who listen to birds sing and watch the wind in the grass on the hill.

And men who can take discipline, can accept the responsibility of being who they are and what they are.

WHEN?

Finish high school for sure.

Know what it is to work for a living.

Solve your draft problem one way or other.

An experience of college can be useful, depending on where you go and what you do while there.

Fundamental abilities are much in order: using a shovel, an axe, a hoe, driving a truck, a tractor.

Fundamental crafts are very salutary: carpentry, bookbinding, printing, machinist, plumbing, cooking, baking, forestry.

Arts and letters are fine: foreign language, classics, Latin, Greek, Hebrew, literature.

Science: a little goes a long way. Nature study: excellent.

The computer world: unknown here.

Travel: fine: Europe, Orient, South America, USA.

Most of us think eighteen is too young, but it has been done, successfully. Also unsuccessfully many times.

We like it if you can listen to music and play some.

We like it if you notice rain, feel the wind, hear the birds, smell the soup.

We like you to be aware, not asleep; alive, not dead; in touch, not gone.

As for drugs, if you've gone too far, this may be tough for you. But here, we feel we do not need them: our culture is not that sick in the monastery.

Granted the horrid state of things today, we still feel that the monastic thing works for those called to it and that you can take it straight and get out of it all it has to offer and that without benefit of artificial stimulus. You ought to have your moral life pretty well in hand by the time you are thinking of a monastery. Sudden conversions are all right, but their depth should be tested.

Monks are sinners, every one, but they all feel too that a man should finish his soup before he goes on to the next course.

A visit to the monastery for a few days is always in order. You can talk with a vocational secretary, the novice master, the abbot. Others too if you like. A day or two in the monastery, a few talks with some of these monks and you ought to know whether the thing is worth carrying any further. Write the guestmaster to have a room for you.

EXCURSUS. A FURTHER ASPECT OF THE MONASTIC CALLING: REFLECTIONS ON AN AMBIGUOUS JOURNEY, AUGUST, 1972.

I am just back from a pilgrimage for peace, from the Monastery here (dedicated to the Mother of God) to the Shrine of the same Holy Mother, in Washington, D. C., by foot. A distance, I guess, of about 225 miles. It took me twelve days. Originally I planned to carry a backpack with full supplies for stopping where I happened to be at the end of each day. But after a few days, what with the combined heat, and the weight of the pack, I had to abandon it and fare as best I could. I stayed two nights in the tent, three nights in rectories of parish priests, and the rest in motels along the way. I went by Route 15, a wandering black-top highway which is less travelled than the major routes and thus more appropriate for walkers. I discovered, however, that highways, even old and wandering ones, make small or no provisions for pedestrians: it was far too dangerous. I do not recommend this mode of travel! I had one rather close call when a car zoomed off the highway (faulty steering mechanism) a few yards behind me.

I managed to say Mass every day, a happy circumstance. And there are few parishes on the route. Twice in the tent, once in the woods, the rest in churches. Priests along the way were most cordial and hospitable, going to considerable trouble for me. Since the pilgrimage had been made public, quite a few knew who I was, many of the drivers waved or made the peace sign. All seemed friendly enough, and I found no hostility at all.

Twenty miles a day seems to have been average, sometimes more, sometimes less. Usually about eight hours walking. I do not walk fast, but with some persistence. I took the dog along (a Dalmatian) for company, protection, and to avoid being offered rides: I got no offers. She enjoyed it all. Since she and I both gathered ticks as we walked along the shoulders of the road, the nights in the tent went mostly to tick-hunting.

The first day (night, actually) was splendid, thirty-five pound pack and all. The next day was tough. The third I could scarcely walk. That's when I got rid of the pack: mailed it ahead. Later, Father Dan drove up to check on me (his idea, and thank the Lord for it), and he moved it further on. He did this twice more. I carried a rain coat and toothbrush, razor, comb (providentially I had been letting my hair get long: it saved my scalp!) and New Testament with Psalms. I had planned to wear a black work scapular as a sign I was a monk, but it was simply too hot.

I reached the outskirts of Washington on the twelfth day. Traffic by then was really dizzy. Those who met me convinced me I had gone far enough and that it would be risky walking further especially with the dog: many highways have scant shoulders or none, and bridges are often very bad, with no place to walk. Friday, I rested and saw the papers for photographs, and Saturday went to the Shrine to offer Mass with two priests and a small group of peace people at the altar of Our Lady of Guadalupe, patroness of the Americas. It was very lovely. A priest and friend drove down from New Jersey to share the Mass. Afterwards we went downstairs for breakfast together. I was not permitted to wear my cowl (it was Thomas Merton's) for Mass, but I did make a "formal" entry into the huge church in my habit with the cowl on. It was enough. Tom was with me.

Though not lacking in belligerence and even violence, I still consider myself a man of peace and have done so all my life: as priest, missionary, and certainly as monk. I look on my whole life as a "peace action." Certainly the contemplative life is rooted in peace with one's self, with one's neighbor, with God. A peace action in the market place seems somewhat superfluous, in that case. Still, peace is having a hard time these days and the more I thought about it, discussed it, the more necessary it seems to me to say something out loud, as it were, as a monk, for the cause of peace. Just to let peace know that we are kin. Sometimes peace people come here to make a little retreat and I once casually mentioned to one of them that I was toying with the idea of walking to Washington as a peace pilgrimage. (Bishop Waters takes a group to the Shrine each year: that gave me the idea—walking seemed to be more monastic!) The reaction was so touching, so overwhelmingly favorable and even pleading that I was really quite shaken. I had no idea that the peace movement was so discouraged and disheartened. Once I got that message, I decided to go through with it. Here in the monastery we had long since agreed that it would be a good thing, but we did nothing about it.

I do not think of it as a Cistercian thing, nor a Gethsemani thing, even, for that matter, an Oxford thing. It was simply a monk saying something for peace in a way that seems to me not out of keeping with his basic life thrust. Certainly a pilgrimage for peace is not alien to our life-style. Not when you think of the mess things are in. And being in a small monastery of an experimental character and thus in a position to try something like this, I felt a certain call of the Spirit to respond to grace. I did not ask my abbot simply because I did not think it fair to do so: I saw no reason to hang the thing around his neck and make him carry it. It seemed to me within our competence, that we should assume responsibility for it.

The ambiguous note of it does not escape me. On the way, for example, a very big and violent dog came out to us on the road and attacked me and the dog with real intent. I had to kick the beast off and with my boots gave him some blows that made him stagger. He then left. I thought: here is your man of peace, your non-violent one in action! In a showdown, see what comes out! I did a lot of thinking about it.

But we deal with mystery. Violence is a mystery because it is rooted in evil somehow, in sin, our common heritage. And the evil influence floats around in us all. It needs little encouragement. Violence breeds violence. And that is why peace is rooted in prayer, in grace. We deal with something far greater, far deeper than we realize. It is a kind of demon driven out only by prayer and fasting. I do not have the answers. I think war is wrong, that violence, whether personal or national or international is wrong. And yet I do not pretend to have answers to obvious difficulties. It is a matter of taking Christ at His word. Taking Him seriously. Living it out as best we can. For if there are monsters in our depths, and there are, there is also the presence of God. And when we touch that, we set free the power of love. Love breeds love. Peace breeds peace. I am not prepared to say how. But as a monk I mean to sow peace, to breed love. Day by day. Somehow or other. As best I can.

When I was in Washington some of my SVD friends took me to task, thought me simplistic, naive. Unrealistic. I had no answers. I just told them what Christ said. What it says on our coins: the Pentagon's motto is not In God We Trust. They do not need Him.

Back of this, of course, is my own fear that we will soon face a terrifying confrontation of Christian and State. Certainly if this country moves further along the road to being a militarist state ruling the world by violent means, or making super-violence a standard technique in international affairs, how can the Christian go along with it? Be a part of it? Support it? Pray for it? These are dark clouds on our sky.

Prayer, then, on a deep level, seems more a duty than ever. We need God's grace and light. But to make that prayer the kind it should be, I think we should have at least some grasp of the awesome dimensions of our situation today. A monk ought to live with an awareness of the real problems and see with a keen vision. He needs the light born of prayer to do that: but he also needs some information.

This pilgrimage was thought of also, I might note, as a call to my fellow monks to the works of peace, to love for their country, their fellow man, expressed primarily in their life of prayer. Our life is one of peace, but perhaps we ought to go to some trouble to make sure this is understood. That people really know where we stand, where our heart is. This is not particularly difficult, nor does it involve our doing anything contrary to our state.

Perhaps difficult times lie ahead. Who knows? Times in which issues will be more clear than they are now, or seem to be. There is no harm in preparing for that now, as much for ourselves that we may be real witnesses to our Christ, as for those who already grasp the dimensions of the conflict and are much disturbed and shaken, and, I would gather, not too comforted by those one would think first to be on hand with solace and strength.

The peace people I met—and I met some—struck me deep and I admire them. Admittedly they flounder in techniques and methods and they know it, yet the scene is very difficult. Few good deeds and few good words are without some ambiguity, and it occurs to me, that the more ardent the word or deed, the more noble and inspired, the more likely is it to be burdened with ambiguity. One can only think of the scandal of the Cross. Or Bethlehem. Or Gethsemani. And even Tabor put them to sleep for fear. But this ambivalent note cannot discourage one.

Certainly the monk's life is ambiguous: he does nothing; he works at the world's problems in the silence and solitude of the desert, a scandal to many. But it is a scandal that does not fool peace people. They are wise to monks. They are up to what they are doing. Party to it. They find in us brothers and kindred spirits.

But I think a little encouragement would help. A hint. A suggestion. A nod. Even a wink. For we wrestle with the same demons, are engaged in the same struggle, same powers of darkness. Washington, for one, is a loud, noisy, dirty city, a lot of frosting over a lot of burned cake. And in and out of it move lots of good people, holy people, serious and sincere people. They can use a little peace and quiet, a little prayer, a little love and hope. And there are many Washingtons. I went to Compline at Saint Anselm's Abbey in the city. Just another visitor. But the place was radiant with peace. It was like a cool drink along a very hot and very long road.

So it was a spiritual trek, even though I prayed very little; I could not. I put all my energy in walking and made steps my psaltery. Besides, it was so very noisy along the highway. But I could think a lot and I did. It was a journey for non-violence, a plea for world peace, a statement against war: this war and all war. It was an Amen to Pope Paul's visit to the UN: War Never Again (does anyone remember?). It was an act of penitence for my own sins of violence in thought and word and deed, as well as for those of our country against how many people. It was a call to prayer for peace and a return to our own hearts where dwells the Spirit of Peace.

So I come home much enriched, much deepened, but filled also with worry and with foreboding. What lies ahead of us? Where will we all meet again? How much longer will we be able to live like this?

Well, there is a God and all things are in His hands. We can live free and without fear if we abide in His will, buoyed up by His grace. Day by day. One step at a time.

This place never looked so sweet and lovely as when I returned to it. It was never so welcome a sight; so radiant a vision. And when I walked into the library and saw there two turtle doves given by a friend while I was away, I was near tears. Two doves, white ones. They coo for peace. I call them Peace and Joy. What a beautiful gift. All day long they quietly speak for peace. And at dawn and at twilight. And in the dark of the night the peacocks scream for help.

The Challenge
of Thomas Merton

Julius Lester

Mr. Lester's books include *To Be a Slave*, a Newbery
Honor Book in 1969 and winner of the Lewis Carroll Shelf
Award and the Nancy Bloch Award. He is also the author
of *Look Out, Whitey, Black Power's Gon' Get Your
Mama; Revolutionary Notes; Search for the New Land;
Long Journey Home: Stories from Black History; The*

*Knee-High Man and Other Tales; The Seventh Son: The
Thoughts and Writings of W. E. B. Du Bois,* and *Two Love
Stories.* With Pete Seeger, he wrote *Folksinger's Guide to
the Twelve String Guitar As Played by Leadbelly.* He is a
lecturer in Black History at the University of Massachusetts.

"I want to be a monk," I said to mother. I don't
remember how old I was. Seventeen, maybe. I can't
even remember where I could have heard of monks or
monasteries in Nashville, Tennessee in the mid-nineteen
fifties, but somehow I had, and the idea of spending my
life in a cloister, praying, singing Gregorian chants,
and studying appealed to my nature much more than
the prospect of working for a living, an enterprise for
which I was morally unfit and totally devoid of talent.

Mother was preparing supper, as she usually was
when I wanted to discuss something serious, and she
did not stop or turn around as she said, "Monks don't
do anything."

"Mother!" I exclaimed in protest. "That's all you
talk about. 'Do!' That's not everything, you know."

"What else is there?" she demanded.

And being only seventeen, I didn't know what to say
and could only conclude that she was right; monks
didn't do anything and in that world into which I was
growing, one was raised and educated to do something
with his life. (America is a nation of doing—digging
minerals from the earth, clearing forests, building cities,
highways, cars, airplanes, inventing miracle drugs,
transplanting organs from one body to another. America is what results when the Puritan work ethic goes
psychotic.)

I was seventeen and everyone wanted to know what

I was going "to do" with my life. Not much, it appeared more and more as I meandered through college, for the early promise I had shown disappeared one day when I asked, of no one in particular, "Who am I?"

The answer came back so quickly that I was almost knocked from my feet: "A nigger!" The society had been trying to get me to believe that for seventeen years, and I'd always found such a definition incomprehensible. What was a nigger? Was it seasonal, like black-eyed peas? Maybe it was the successor to the Edsel, or something between the woofer and tweeter on my hi-fi. Whatever it was, I'd wait until the price went down before getting one.

Rejecting that answer to my question, a long and deep silence descended, swathing me so tightly that sometimes I had to struggle to breathe. "Who am I?" I demanded to know, and the mere question was a challenge to God, because I'd learned in church every Sunday that I was a child of God, created in His own image, and that Jesus had died so that I might be redeemed from sin. To ask "Who am I" was to reject that Christian dogma and confront God directly: "If You know who I am, then speak. If You are indeed my Creator and in You and only in You will I find meaning, reveal Yourself. Do it in a burning bush, or a pillar of fiery clouds, or a red MG, if there are no bushes around."

But God, I learned, is not a dog, who comes when requested. Despite the theologians, I think God is choosy about what prayers He answers and what petitions He will grant. When you pray, God has St. Peter tap your phone; He looks through your dossier and sees what your soul has been doing behind the veil of your *persona,* and if He thinks you've paid your dues, if

He thinks you have walked in the path of righteousness, maybe He'll listen to what you have to say.

So it appeared to me as I stumbled through the desert of myself, searching for the am-of-my-I, searching for the I-of-my-am. St. John of the Cross calls it *la noche oscura*—the dark night of the soul—wherein one is made to know his miniscule finiteness in every fibre and corpuscle of his being. Mine lasted for almost three years, until God allowed me to see Him as I rode on a train from Los Angeles, California to San Francisco. I had seen the ocean many times, but this once I saw it and the mountains that rose from the rocky beach at the edge of the sea and knew that this was the "I am that I am" and so was I. "My me is God," said St. Catherine of Genoa, and Meister Eckhart, frustrated and angry at the inadequacy of language, was driven to cry, "I am God!" And that morning of June 10, 1959, I knew that I was, too. Having taken the risk of revealing Himself, God once again disappeared, reluctant to trust His being in the hands of a mere mortal, having been mistreated and misused so often throughout history. He retreated to see what I would do with my knowledge of who I was.

I became a seagull, flashing white as I soared, dipping over the curling ocean. I became the sky, sparkling in glitters of blue over the world. I became All and each step I took was the most graceful pirouette ever done by a mere mortal.

But the ecstasy which follows release from *la noche oscura* does not last long, particularly when one is a senior in college, and whether or not he knows who he is, he must find something "to do" with his life (as if it were a ball which must be bounced or hit, as if a life were a tract of beautiful land, which cannot be allowed to shine beneath the sun, but must be turned into a Disneyland). It must have been around this time that I came upon Thomas Merton. I can't recall, because looking back it appears that as long as I have been, there was Thomas Merton. I don't even remember whether I read *The Seven Storey Mountain* first or something else. But it is of little consequence. I came to Merton and the idea of becoming a monk was planted in me once again. After all, if one has been blessed by seeing the face of God, it is his duty thereafter to devote his life to God. There is no more pure and direct way of doing so than in a life of contemplation.

Merton's collection of essays, *Disputed Questions*, was a startling revelation to me about monastic life. The first essay was about Pasternak and *Dr. Zhivago*, a *cause célèbre* in the West in 1960 as Solzhenitsyn is now. I was surprised that a man who had been cloistered for twenty years or so knew so much about the dynamics of the "outside" world. This was no sanctimonious priest mouthing pieties, but a man more involved than most who lived in the world, more astute in his observations and insights than the more recognized social commentators. (After all, how can anyone really take Max Lerner seriously?) There was a purity in Merton's vision and literary style which a young twenty-one-year-old like me would find appealing, because the young listen only to those who have pure ideals. (And the danger with the young is that the purity is more important than the content of the ideals. Jesus freaks and Weathermen are the same people, masquerading as dissimilar ones.) The pure idealism of Merton was not expressed in simplistic dictums, which would only have resulted in his becoming the focus for a cult. No. He challenged one with a clear statement of an ideal that could only be reached through agonizing spiritual work. He told us what our duty was, but gave us no formulas by which to fulfill it.

. . . our job is to love others without stopping to inquire whether or not they are worthy. That is not our business and, in fact, it is nobody's business. What we are asked to do is to love; and this love itself will render both ourselves and our neighbors worthy if anything can ("The Power and Meaning of Love").

How much I wanted to rush off to the Abbey of Gethsemani, don my cowl and sit in Merton's class for novitiates. And I would have had I not been required to join the Catholic Church, which always struck me as being akin to enlisting in the Army. I could not accept any authority over my life.

Though it would be some while before I was sure, my way was in and of the world. I was not only prey to the appetites of the flesh, I was loathe to give them up. Even on those days when I thought that I could be a Catholic, I knew that I could never be celibate. And not even Merton was able to convince me otherwise. The Lord had bestowed upon me an almost infinite capacity to lust, and to deny it would be to deny myself. I could not understand salvation through denial. Salvation came through fulfillment of self.

So I entered the world, the arena of "doing," where there was no place for a contemplative in search of a form for his life. I would have to make my own form, and I was happy to read an essay of Merton's confirming the desirability of the contemplative life in a secular environment.

. . . true contemplation is inseparable from life and from the dynamism of life—which includes work, creation, production, fruitfulness and above all *love*. Contemplation is not to be thought of as a separate department of life, cut off from all man's other interests and superseding them. It is the very fulness of a fully integrated life. It is the crown of life and of all life's activities. . . .

. . . what we need are "contemplatives" outside the cloister and outside the rigidly fixed patterns of religious life—contemplatives in the world of art, letters, education, and even politics. This means a solid integration of one's work, thought, religion, and family life and recreations in one vital harmonious unity with Christ at its center ("Poetry and Contemplation").

There was, perhaps, no more contradictory time to become a contemplative than 1960. The sit-in movement had begun and the social revolution of the 60's had begun. I held myself apart from the ferment around me, suspicious of its ability to make significant change. I listened to the platitudes of Martin Luther King, Jr. and was not convinced that he knew what Merton knew. Non-violence was a tool for the *contemplative*, not the political organizer, and Dr. King seemed to be a product of libraries and Bayard Rustin as opposed to any kind of inner struggle to attain Being. He commanded us to love our enemies, but that is not possible when a people do not love themselves. Black people could not be soldiers of *satyagraha;* they could only be passive resisters. (In his last public appearance King said that he had been to the mountaintop and seen the promised land, and though it was an inspired use of Biblical imagery, it confirmed the feeling I'd always had about Dr. King: He saw himself as Moses come to lead the children to the promised land. And I tried to imagine Gandhi saying he had been to the mountaintop, and I couldn't. Gandhi would have looked puzzled and said, "No, but let me tell you about Hell," because it is in hell fire that the soul is tempered and refined and made ready to do God's work.) I did not sit-in or freedom-ride, because, even though Dr. King talked about redemption through suffering, I could not feel love vibrating from him, only quasi-religious rhetoric uttered in the dulcet tones of a sophisticated Baptist minister. Dr. King was wrapped in the aura of the spiritual, but his essence was political. The right use of non-violence demands a spiritual leader. Merton made a distinction between "the non-violence of the weak" and "the non-violence of the strong," and he defined the former as using "the language of power. It is a different method of expressing one's will to power." Non-violence of the strong was "not for power but truth. . . . It does not say 'We shall overcome' so much as 'This is the day of the Lord, and whatever may happen to us, *He* shall overcome.'"

Of course, in the early sixties, none of the above was clear in my mind. I just knew that the civil rights movement did not resonate with the bell-like tones of the soul's purity and I stayed away, living as best I could a life of study and contemplation in New York while working at various odd jobs until I decided that even to work at something which did not bring me closer to God was blasphemy. My last job was with the welfare department, and when I quit in April of 1963, I put my physical well-being in God's hands: "Listen. If You want me to be about Your work, You pay the rent." And perhaps God liked my audaciousness, because He hasn't missed a month in ten years (though He does cut it rather close sometimes).

By now I was married and in a few years would be a father, which truly brings one into the world. Sometimes I think it is easier to live with God than it is with another human being, particularly one who does not understand the contemplative life. Marriage is a perverse institution anyway, particularly when most of us think that just because we love someone we can live with them. The two are not necessarily related, but it took me eight years to finally realize that.

I, the monk without a monastery, married a Marxist-Leninist without a Russia, someone who could see the class struggle in a bowl of Rice Krispies. Our values were very different and she was so much better at expressing hers than I was mine. I felt no need to convince her of the truths I had learned, but for her there was only one truth—Marxism-Leninism. And because I conceded that possibly she might be right, I slowly found myself viewing the world with political eyes, seeing "the oppressed" where before I'd just seen people, seeing the "ruling class" where before I'd just seen *rich* people. It was a slow, subtle transformation and without realizing it, I forgot Merton and became a part of my times.

I joined SNCC and believed that the revolution had come. I traveled to college campuses and spoke on the necessity for revolution and wrote articles and books in an attempt to articulate an ideology for revolution. I believed that a revolution was necessary, but I also knew that ultimately the revolution had to be spiritual. However, I was convinced that it was possible to inject the radical political movement with a spiritual essence, and it was to that end that I wrote.

... the revolutionary knows that to change the institutions he must change himself. He and his comrades must become new men, for it is from new men that the new institutions will come which, in turn, will create the new society.

Those words are from the introduction to my *Revolutionary Notes,* and that phrase "new men" was Che Guevara's. But it was also Merton's, for he had titled one of his books *The New Man* (and it is not a romantic idealization of Che or an insult to Merton to say that the two were spiritual brothers).

The revolution I talked and wrote about had only one purpose: to transform humanity into vehicles for God. I kept His name out of my writings, knowing that the mere sight of it would mean I would be unread by many whom I wanted to reach. But the word is not the thing. "Revolution does not mean us against them," I wrote in the midst of the Newark rebellion of 1968. "The revolutionary is a midwife seeking to give birth to the full potential of man. Involved in that most difficult of all births is our fighting against them, but let us not confuse that fight with Revolution. . . . One can never say that he is a revolutionary. One is only in a constant state of becoming revolutionary, of becoming more human."

As long as I could believe that those who read me understood, even subconsciously, that I was talking about oneness with God, I could continue to be a part of "the movement." But I deluded myself, for I had not realized that what we called the revolutionary movement had erred with its very first step—the enunciation of Black Power. I was caught up in it, too, and not until the transition was made from the slogan "Black Power" to "Power to the People" did I begin to question where we were going. I didn't want any part of a revolution whose aim was the acquisition of power. Power could not be used compassionately, by an individual or some mystical grouping called "the people." Power was unequivocally evil.

I increasingly realized that I had articulated a concept of revolution which bore little relation to the reality of revolution. By the winter of 1969 I knew, in a frightening moment of insight, that my life would be no different or safer if Eldridge Cleaver occupied the White House. Indeed, it might be worse. He talked of love, but I could feel no compassion in him, no challenge to his followers to walk in the path of Being. And I was afraid.

I continued to write and speak. I had to, because I was unable to confront myself with the truth of what I saw happening within "the movement," as people raised clenched fists high into the air and shouted "Power to the People." My mind would play a strange trick and I would see outstretched arms and flattened hands and hear "Seig Heil!"

The confrontation with myself finally came when I accepted an invitation from Jim Holloway to speak at Berea College, where he taught. It was an overcast day when I arrived, and as we drove from the airport, I slumped in the seat and let the Kentucky hills wrap me in their quiet. And perhaps it was something in the peace of the hills that caused me to remember that the Abbey of Gethsemani was nearby. A few questions got Jim to reveal that he had known Merton and I regretted that I had come to the area after he had died. But talking of him for the first time in years brought me faint whiffs of something I'd once loved to partake of, and there was a moment of wishing that I could return to it, that somehow my life had veered from where I had wanted it to go.

Once we arrived on campus, I was introduced to some black students and put in their care until I spoke that evening. The black students closed around me like foxes around a rabbit and I didn't know what to do, there being no briar patch to dash into. I had become increasingly uneasy speaking at colleges, because as I stood before the audiences, looked out and saw the black students seated in a section at the front and the whites behind them, I knew that I was supposed to be the voice for those black students. I was to apply the whip to "whitey," to be the avenging voice of the race. I could never do it. Of course, anger coursed through me as it does all blacks, but that anger did not comprise the totality of my being. I persisted in believing that whites were human, in spite of themselves, but I had internalized too much Merton to ever regard them as anything more or less than pitiful mortals like myself in need of as much love as I myself was. Love was God's language, and while I might find myself incapable of loving at a given moment, the attempt to love was always within my grasp, and the one thing I could not do was to refuse to make the attempt. As I stood before those college audiences and felt the pain of the black students, felt their need to live through me, to have me be their symbol and their spokesman, I felt they were asking me to refuse to treat whites as human beings and treat them as whites, as objects to be assailed with the pain of black lives. I refused.

That gray day at Berea I felt particularly trapped, because I wanted to sit with the white students, too. They were southerners and that meant we shared a history and that our lives were inseparable. But the black students surrounded me like Secret Service men, not protecting me from assassination, but unconscious agents of the act themselves.

That evening as we walked toward the chapel where I was to speak, a white girl approached me. She hugged her arms tightly around her, as if she were forever alone with no one to hold her but herself. When she spoke to me, her eyes fluttered up to mine and down to the ground quickly. There was a slight quaver in her voice, which was not shyness, but fear. She was afraid as she looked at me and saw a black person phalanxed by unsmiling, hard-eyed young blacks. And her look told me that she thought I was one of them. And I didn't know what to do, not wanting to make the black students feel that I was rejecting them, yet wanting to let the girl know that who she saw was not me. I wanted to ask her to unclasp her arms and throw them around me so that I could cry for what was happening to me and to her and to our poor, pathetic world.

To whatever she asked me, I made a joke, knowing that the only weapon I had was to make her laugh, but my joke bounced against her fear and plopped at my feet like a dead fish. She looked at me, bewildered, muttered something and hurried away.

I spoke that evening, masking the deep pain I felt at having been unable to communicate with someone who had wanted to communicate with me, and hoped that she heard what I said, because I spoke to her that evening. But afterwards, she left without speaking to me again. And that night I resolved to stop speaking publicly until I had the spiritual strength not to let myself be captured by black students who used me as a club in their battle against anguish. The black students who invited me to their campuses did not want *me*. They wanted their version of me, which bore no similarity to the reality of the am-of-my-I. Equally, the white students who were so relieved that I did not curse them out for being white assumed that I was not like the black students who rejected them. Neither group could understand that I was both of them, in more ways than they knew.

Merton speaks of "the man who is fully born," as one who is "identified with everybody" and is "all things to all men . . . able to experience their joys and sufferings as his own, without however becoming dominated by them." Whether or not I qualified, it was an ideal I tried to live by. To be "fully born" was to be vulnerable, to be open to the pain of others to the extent of making that pain one's own, and when I stood before those audiences, it was not to bring them a "message" but to be vulnerable and let my words come from my vulnerability and touch theirs. (Any speaker has the same experience if he is not as concerned with what he is going to say as he is with to whom he is saying it.)

The change had begun when I left Berea the next day, and before the year was out I would have ceased to call myself a revolutionary. If revolution was the overthrow of governments, I wanted no part of it. Once again God used Jim Holloway to speak to me. Jim called and asked me to write an essay about Jacques Ellul. I'd never heard of him, but I said O.K., and that summer of 1969 I read through all of Ellul's works, and particularly in *The Political Illusion* I could feel myself coming back to the beginning, back to the person I had been almost ten years before when I had gone into the world, a contemplative without a cell.

Ellul affirmed the renewed contact I had had with Merton through Jim and those Kentucky hills Merton had so often looked on. When Ellul said that a political solution to a political problem was only a reinforcement of the problem, I knew that I had been right back in 1960 when I had told friends who were sitting-in: "Oh, you may desegregate the lunch counters, but you won't really change anything."

It was to be another two years, though, before I returned wholly to the point from which I had started. I had to confront myself in the void which had been created when I ceased to live within the context of "the movement," which had been my entire life for four years. At the same time my marriage was hurtling toward its inevitable dissolution. I was thirty-one and had thought my life would be a harmonious whole by that time, but there it was, coming apart like a sweater bought at a bargain basement sale. But it was Emerson who pointed out, "God will not have His work made manifest by cowards," and I have the feeling that, periodically, God wants to see what we're made of, those of us in whom He risks Himself. He sets out to destroy us, pushing us to our limits, and if we survive, He is surprised and gratified, and without bothering to say, "Congratulations," He gives us more work to do.

Somehow I survived the disintegration of my life, and with the pieces lying around me I began again. And there, almost as if I had summoned him by a magical incantation, was Thomas Merton. *The New York Times Sunday Book Review* asked me to review the first of his posthumous works, *Contemplation in a World of Action.* To me it is his most eloquent book, for in it he speaks more directly of the contemplative life than he ever had before, and in so doing, distilled the wisdom gained from his own contemplative existence.

The monk is not defined by his task, his usefulness. In a certain sense he is supposed to be "useless" because his mission is not to *do* this or that job but to *be* a man of God. He does not live in order to exercise a specific function; his business is life itself.... Monasticism aims at the cultivation of a certain *quality* of life, a level of awareness, a depth of consciousness, an area of transcendence and of adoration which are not usually possible in an active secular existence. ...

But this time I did not long to enter a monastery, because the challenge of Merton could be met in "an active secular existence." The task was to first free one's self from the disease of doing and painfully make his way toward Being.

... a true and mature identity does not consist in the ability to give a final solution to everything—as if the "mature person" were one for whom there were no longer any mysteries or any scandals. We discover our identity when we accept our place and our way in the midst of persons and things, in a historical situation, that we do not have to completely understand. We simply see that it is our own place and decide to live in it, for better or for worse. In the light of this simple and primordial acceptance, a natural consent, an obedience to reality that is already analogous to the obedience of faith, we can finally "be ourselves."

My task, upon which I had already embarked before reading *Contemplation in a World of Action,* was to no longer accept the definition of black which had been bestowed upon me. Race and culture were abstractions, emphasizing the differences between people and allowing no means of letting others into our selves. The black movement of which I had been so integral a part may have been a political advance, but it was a spiritual retreat, an acceptance of the values of the slave masters. It was they who had conceived and defined black and placed certain values upon it. To change those values and definitions from the negative ones of the slave masters to positive ones (Black is beautiful) was to participate actively in turning one's self into an abstraction, an object, a thing, a nonperson. And between two objects, there is no possibility of an I-Thou relationship.

To be free I had to cease to be black and be the am-of-my-I. My racial identity was a part of that, but only a part. It was the equating of racial identity with the whole of the personal self which turned people into objects. Freedom came only from selfhood becoming Selfhood.

What is meant by identity? . . . We are talking about one's own authentic and personal beliefs and convictions, based on experience of one's self as a person, experience of one's ability to choose and reject even good things which are not relevant to one's own life. . . . Identity in this deep sense is something that one must create for himself by choices that are significant and that require a courageous commitment in the face of anguish and risk. . . . It means having a belief one stands by; it means having certain definite ways of responding to life, of meeting its demands of loving other people, and, in the last analysis, of serving God. In this sense, identity is one's witness to truth in one's life.

Merton challenged me to be myself at a time when my people demanded that I be black, but to define myself as "black" was to do nothing but invert the "nigger" American society had tried so hard to make me believe I was. The challenge of Merton was the perpetual struggle to vulnerability.

To love our brother we must first respect him in his own authentic reality, and we cannot do this if we have not attained to a basic self-respect and mature identity ourselves.

And I am more and more convinced that there isn't anything else to living but that. Love is impossible without a continual confrontation with the self, without the achieving of a basic level of identity. "Love," Merton writes. "Is it an act? Or, is it a happening?" And there he touches it precisely. We conceive of love as something "to do." It isn't. It is an emanation of Being, happening because we are living from the still point within ourselves, because we have learned "to wait upon the Lord."

"Whoever dwells among wolves," wrote that Christian pilgrim, Nikos Kazantzakis, "must be a lamb—and not care a jot if they eat him!" Like the lamb, we must be still, dumb before the impending slaughter, looking upon the descending butcher's blade with round, wide eyes, understanding what is about to happen, and if it must, it must. It is not important. This is not to be construed as apathy in the reign of Richard the King. No, but let us understand: Kings are not dethroned by peasant revolts. Kings are only dethroned when no one needs to create them. Let us understand that governments are our creations, not God's, because once we stand on "our own feet before God and the world," as Merton writes, "and take full responsibility" for our own lives, it will be impossible for governments to exist.

Then, what are we to do? Nothing, for the world is about to expire from our doing. "Be still and let Him do some work."

A Greek Tragedy—
American Style

Heslip Lee

"Happy" Lee, a Baptist preacher, is Assistant to the Dean, School of Urban Life, Georgia State University (Atlanta). He has been Deputy Director of Atlanta University's Multi-Purpose Training Center; Urban Affairs Specialist at North Carolina State University (Raleigh); Vice-President for Development, Shaw University, North Carolina;

124

Executive Director, Virginia Council on Human Relations; and consultant to numerous foundations and federal and private agencies on education, urban affairs and racial problems.

For the record, my name is *Lee*. You spell it just as in Robert E. Lee. I'm from Polk County, Georgia, and I'm a Baptist. There isn't supposed to be any harm in either of these three things. These things have served me well, along with being a redneck from Georgia, born in a tenant farmer's home, delivered by a midwife. The doctor in our area had several thousand acres and many tenants—approximately half black, half white. He was away in the legislature when I was born (under the sign of Pisces), so I was delivered by a midwife in this tenant farmer's home. We could put everything we had on two 2-horse wagons and move it all in a half day. The fact is, we did just that. Every year. So when I was seventeen years old, we had moved eighteen times, always looking for just that better plot of land which would grow more cotton. I didn't know there was anything to do but raise cotton and plow jackasses until I was grown and married. I never dreamed of being able to do anything other than the thing my parents had done, which was to raise cotton.

This is the background I want to use for "A Modern Greek Tragedy—American Style, In Living Color." You do not have to read Shakespeare or Homer to find tragedies. We have modern day ones. I want to consider my subject as nothing more than what I would call an existential experience of a boy born in the twentieth century, in the land of the free and home of the brave, who was locked into a culture, into a system that deprived him of any vision or courage or any hope of performing work or vocation in the twentieth century except within a structure which excluded all those Americans who were different from us. I have also found that same prison, only in different forms, everywhere I have gone since.

I was born in a three-county-world. I say "three-county-world" because that's as much of the world as we knew about when I was growing up. It had about a ten-mile radius. In that world, we had an entire system that gave us our world-view and our life-style. I'm not making this up, and what I'm going to describe is something that is happening in this very age in America. That is why I call it, Greek tragedy, American-style.

That world-view taught me from the time I was born to despise Catholics. Catholics were going to take over the Church of the world, they were the anti-Christs, there was something dreadfully wrong with them. The fact that I never met a Catholic until I was twenty-eight years old didn't matter and I felt myself to have been fortunate because of this fact.

I was also taught to exclude from *my* world-view and life-style all Jews. They were hoarding all the money on the earth. If we didn't watch them closely they would soon take over the economy of the whole world. In my three-country world we had one Jewish family living in the county seat. They ran a clothing store. We were taught that if we ever went in there we ought to remember to hold our hands on our pocketbook because otherwise they would take our money right off us. We didn't even know that the word "Jew" was a noun. We always thought it was a verb, since the only way we used it was to go in their store and

"Jew-them-down." Guess what their names were? *Williams!*

And I was also taught by my world-view that all Yankees were bad. They lived north of some imaginary line, wouldn't eat greasy food, had no morals, and all of them practiced crime. The *only* Yankees I ever heard about when I was growing up was that bunch of them who decided to take a tour of my Southland, led by a man named Sherman. He came by way of Atlanta and burned everything in his path until he got a look at the sea. So, there was something bad wrong with all those Yankees who lived north of some imaginary line.

My world-view excluded all foreigners. It was perfectly all right to go to war against any foreigner, at any time. It was all right to fight the Germans under the Kaiser or Hitler, the Italians under Mussolini, the Japs under Tojo, and for that matter, to fight any foreigner at any time and any place, because all foreigners were our enemies. They were not like us, we were not like them. We should always get our enemies before they got us. Good old Uncle Sam always told us when to go after them. This part of my world-view pervades my Southland to such a degree that even today, where do you find the greatest pro-war spirit in the country? *Any* war? Against *any* foreigner? It is in my Southland. Do you remember when Mr. Johnson got in bad trouble about the Vietnam war, and sent Secretary of State Rusk to have a gigantic pro-war rally? Do you remember where he went? To Atlanta, Georgia. Anyone who takes issue with the method or numbers of Vietnamese that one of our Southern boys, named Calley, killed is non-Christian and un-American.

The "Feds" were also part of the conspiracy of enemies in my world-view. If the federal government didn't "get us" today, they'd "get us" tomorrow, because their leadership was made up of Catholics, Jews, Yankees, and foreigners. This group had a conspiracy never to elect a Southerner as President. They even came around once every ten years to find out how many chickens, dogs and kids we had. They were part of that great evil conspiracy which was after us and would get us one way or another.

Another enemy was the labor unions. They were the enemy, they were gestapo people, communists, the scum of the earth. *All* labor unions. *No* exceptions. They were out to undercut our free enterprise system.

Now I could go on and on with this. I could tell you how my world-view excluded all Republicans, communists, socialists, atheists, Japs, Wops, Dagoes, half-breeds, radiclibs, etc. But you know where I'm heading because of what I've *not* mentioned. There was one group that was worse than all these groups put together and that was *The Niggers!* The Niggers were a thousand, thousand times worse than any and all these other groups combined.

All this was part of how my world-view programmed me for my life's work. I guess you could say my vocation, my calling. And that is why I call it a modern Greek tragedy—American style, in living color. For any boy to be born in the twentieth century and to have his world-view and life-style dominated by the *exclusion* of Catholics, Yankees, foreigners, Japanese, Italians, Socialists and Blacks is exactly just that. No greater tragedy could ever be conceived. It was hard, even in my three-county-world, to carry it off, so we had to practice some discrimination. For example, if you had to have any relationship with any of these enemies, it was better to relate to a Catholic than to a Nigger. I even had a cousin who married a Catholic during the Second World War. He couldn't live with her as his wife in my home county. She wouldn't eat meat on Friday, she had all these strange habits that became the conversational piece of our whole family. Since he couldn't live with her in Polk County, Georgia, he took her back to Philadelphia, Pennsylvania, to live. But at least he could marry her and live with her in some sort of normal relationship in some section of the country (even though it told us something about the Yankees that they would let them live together). But he married her and we didn't kill them.

Also, if you had to have dealings with the enemies, it was better to deal with Jews than Niggers, or Yankees than Niggers, or foreigners than Niggers, even if he was a Black foreigner. Consider this: my great Southern Baptist Convention has been sending out missionaries to Africa for a hundred years to baptize black folk in Africa, and to live with them, minister to them, love them, work with them. Then they'd bring the missionary back home, and every Baptist church in the Association would fight over who was going to get that missionary on Sunday to give his "Report." He'd get up and tell us how many black folk he'd loved and how many he'd baptized and how many he'd ministered to, while the women would sit there and cry and the men would pour hatfuls of money to send more Southern Baptist missionaries to Africa to minister to the black folk. *But keep it over there. Don't ever bring it over here.* Niggers are the greatest enemy.

A time came in my life when I took seriously what they had me singing in that Baptist church—standing on a box when I was five years old—"Red and Yellow,

Black and White, they are precious in God's sight."
"In Christ there is no East or West, etc." Yet my fellow
Southern Baptists got jittery when I wanted to break
down the things that kept us from all being "precious
in his sight" *together*. Many wrote me out of their lives.
I have brothers-in-law who refused to come to my
father-in-law's house when I went back home.

To support and undergird this world-view there was
an ideology which was very simple. Since we had no
education, no money, no access to anything, we needed
a simple way of looking at life. What really supplied
this was . . . *Christianity!* I would call it Greek dualism,
but they called it—and they still call it—Christianity.
It was a neat little set of either/or schemes, and it provided the way we looked at everything. You were either
going to heaven, or you were going to hell. You were
either right, or wrong. You were either good, or bad.
You were either saved, or lost. You were either in, or
out. And on and on. Everything was either/or; black/
white. Where do you get the most editorials against the
United Nations (made up of foreigners who want to
talk before they start shooting)? Or communists?
Or Blacks? or American Jews? Or Castro? From our
Southerners who know only one way of dealing with
the enemy and that is to get him before he gets you.
There is no other way to deal with the enemy.

The thing that was the clincher in our world-view
was that it was a virtue to be poor. The fact that we
were poor was our meal ticket to heaven. More of the
Greek dualism: things were all bad down here and
were all good up in heaven. Our songs reflected
this, "We labor and toil as we linger below, but think
of the home over there!" "Some glad morning I'll fly
away!" "In the sweet by and by!" Everything that was

good was in the other world and down here you accepted your fate, especially the fact that you were poor. If anyone questioned it he was getting uppity and running the risk of missing heaven.

And of course all of this world-view was wrapped up and undergirded not only by religion, but by politics, the economy, the social structure, and the educational system. The *whole system* put together this world-view that dominated my three-county-world. We might have rationalized it by saying that we didn't build the system with it's world-view, we inherited it. And I grant that. But it was a rough inheritance and had built-in perpetuation.

When I was 28 years old, with a wife and three children, I decided to move out of the three-county world and its world-view and life-style. While I was preparing to go to college, and after I did, my family and friends held prayer meetings for me for several months. Two days before I enrolled my daddy woke me up at 5:00 in the morning, stood at my bed and cried his eyes out, saying that one hour earlier as he was walking around his barn, an angel stood in his path and God showed him that if I left my old daddy and the farm and my raising, God was going to take my children in death and it was his duty to warn me of this.

But I went anyway, to a Baptist university about 150 miles away. I didn't even know what the word "matriculate" meant. I practically wore out a Webster's Collegiate Dictionary by the end of the first semester. It had been as natural for me to use a singular verb with a plural subject, or vice versa, as drinking water. I didn't know what I wanted to "major" in. I wound up "majoring" in philosophy. I discovered some people who began for the first time in my life to question my three-county world-view. I lived through all this without any traumatic experiences. I was like a bird that had been turned out of a cage. I got so obsessed with meeting new people and facing new ideas and making some sense out of the meaning of life that I forgot to take enough courses in English and Speech and wound up not knowing how to be the professional preacher I thought I might be. I moved out of my three-county world-view, and into one a bit larger, one that covered the Southland.

After I finished college I decided that since I was going to take eight years out of the middle of my life to give to education, I ought to go to a graduate school outside the culture in which I was raised. When I decided to do that, I learned a great lesson about the world-view of others in America today. For when I said, "I'm going to New York to grad school."..., well, My God! everybody jumped on my neck and said, "Happy, good God, man! the world is larger than three counties in north Georgia: your family was wrong, it's larger than *that*. But it isn't as large as you think it is," They were saying that there is a line up there and if you go beyond it, you'll be ruined. Stay in one of our traditional schools. Now, I wasn't dealing with people who had had only a third grade education, or people who had never been 60 miles from home or had never owned an automobile or a radio or who held a three-county world-view. I was dealing with people with degrees—AB's, and MA's, and BD's and LLB's and MD's. And I realized that.... My God! the people in my three-county-world aren't so outdated after all. These supposedly educated people are simply drawing their circle to include thirteen southeastern states instead of three counties in Georgia, but they're operating from the same set of presuppositions as my family and friends. In fact, it was worse with those people, because they believed they had become *educated*. They had the degree. They had the certification. They'd been through the process and the system. But they had become crystalized, insulated, and self-assured. Their world-view was even more limited because it was backed up by all their sophistication and degrees which undergirded and fortified their prejudices.

While I was in graduate school, my family came to see me. It was the first time my father and mother had even been more than sixty miles from home. My father and mother, my sister and her husband and four children, loaded up from Cedartown, Georgia, in their best Sunday clothes, and drove twenty-seven hours straight through to Rochester, N. Y. (so they wouldn't have to stop anywhere and run the risk of dealing with any of the enemies up there). They came to see their son and brother who was in school in New York. But my father had every intention of not having one thing to do with any Yankee while they were there. They were just going to slip in, sit down in my house for a week, and slip back home to Polk County, Georgia. But it so happened that my little boy got his finger clipped off on a bicycle the day after they got here, and I had to stay in the hospital with him for two days. And you know, those Damn Yankees brought in food —eggs, cakes, meat, pies—and my daddy had to meet them at the door. "Oh, you're Happy's father, its good to have you up here!" And he *had* to talk to them. After I got back from the hospital, the Yankees took my daddy out to the biggest farm he'd ever seen in his life, in the Geneseo Valley, and he rode on the biggest tractor he'd ever seen in his life, during hay season, where baled hay was so thick on the ground that he could walk on the bales without once touching the ground. I didn't see much of him anymore the rest of the week, except at night. When he got in the car to leave for home, his last words were, "These are the finest folk I've ever met in my life." Today, the neighbors in Polk County tell me that when somebody talks about Yankees, he'll say, "Now, wait. There's one group of them that's different." That happened to my daddy in one week: in *one* experience of *one* redneck out of Georgia, and he was able to sit down and talk with a bunch of Damn Yankees and come away saying that these were the finest folk he'd ever seen! This is part of the meaning of my Modern Greek tragedy, American Style—that our jobs and our vocations seem to be servants of institutions and structures and systems that continue to isolate us from each other. If in one week my daddy—who has been a segregationist, fundamentalist, Goldwater, George Wallace, Lester Maddox supporter all his life—could find that a group of Yankees were the "finest folk" he'd ever met . . . Well, My God! How simple can it be to remove myths?

I finished graduate school, and have worked all around my Southland since then. I've travelled quite a bit, and what I have found is that most Americans have a world-view and a life-style that is just as rigid, just as dogmatic, just as exclusive of others, and just as hateful as the one I first mentioned in my three-county world. We have developed a world-view that is so powerful that *all* our institutions support it, and feed into it and upon it. And the tragic thing about the Greek tragedy, American-style—the really tragic thing —is that this world-view is the same, whether it is in the three-county world in north Georgia or a thirteen state view of Southern Baptists, or a segregationist white supremacy view or a separatist Black supremacy view, or a Love It or Leave It view, or a Harvard and Yale and P.S. 421 view, or a White House and Congressional view in Washington. Each view is built to support and accept some Americans and exclude others.

I believe something is very wrong with our social system in the 70's when we have made "Law and Order" the national policy that determines everything we do, on every level, national, state, and local. We are all for "Law and Order!" But look at what we mean by it. We primarily mean by it, keep the Blacks and others we may not accept in their place. Whether it is Washington, D.C. or Atlanta, Georgia. Law and Order means *you people stay where I think you ought to be*. We are eighteen years from a law interpreted by the highest part of our system which weighed our educational program in the balances and said it was found wanting and had to go. It said separate education for blacks and whites was unequal, unconstitutional, and had to go. Yet eighteen years later we find the system —political, social, and economic—exerting all its efforts, on all levels—national, state, and local—to defy Law and Order, to declare, as the President did, a "moratorium" on Law and Order that concerned equal education. When we yell Law and Order we don't mean the 1954 Supreme Court decision, The 1964 Civil Rights Law, The 1965 Voting Rights Law or the 1968 Housing Law. There's something wrong with us when we have exerted every bit of energy we could muster in this country to do everything *but* be a nation of Law and Order when it concerns bringing into the system *all* Americans. Every Law and Order speech today, from the President and the Vice-President on down ignores the fact that the real law breakers in this country are those who run the educational systems, the political systems and the housing industry from planners, to builders, to financiers, to realtors.

Recently I was visiting my parents and heard Herman Talmadge give a Law and Order Speech on the radio. I asked my mother to be quiet for just a few moments so I could enjoy the surprise of knowing that Herman was for Law and Order. And she says, "Oh, Herman has *always* been for Law and Order. We gotta stop these niggers from rioting and burning this country down." And I said, "Just hold it a minute. I thought we were going to talk about Law and Order." And she repeats what she had just said. So I said, "We have a 1968 Housing Law approved by the Congress and the Senate and signed by the President. It is the law of the land. Are you for that law?" She says, "No sir! My God doesn't intend for me to live by it." So I said, "Now you have brought God in and I thought you and I were going to discuss whether you and I and Herman Talmadge were for Law and Order. For ten years, Mama, I heard you damn Dr. Martin Luther King because you said he picked the laws that he was going to abide by and ignored those he didn't want to abide by. Now, you're telling me you're going to do the same thing, stoop to use his methods, and say what he said also, that 'your God don't intend for you to live by certain laws.' "

Well, my mother can't deal with this. But neither can my society. We are as locked in as a nation in a world-view that is tighter and more pervasive and stronger than the one with which I began in my three-county world, because there is really nothing in our system and institutions that has shown the strength to challenge it.

It becomes all right to pick a token Black to display on T.V. for one political party, but wrong for the other party to set a quota to bring Blacks into the political decision-making process. It was right to gerrymander school district lines and political congressional district lines to keep Blacks out of schools and politics. But it suddenly became wrong to gerrymander the same lines to bring Blacks into the system. It was right to bus Blacks twenty or more miles to schools to keep them away from our children and better schools and facilities, but suddenly it is wrong to bus anyone two blocks to bring Blacks into dialogue, communication and the educational process with other Americans.

That is why in order to talk about vocations in this country today we must begin by understanding our modern Greek Tragedy, American Style, Live, On Stage And Screen In Living Color.

What Does a
Freedom Fighter Do?

Diane Nash

Diane Nash is community organizer for the Wesley Memorial United Methodist Church, Harvey, Illinois. She was active with the Student Non-Violent Coordinating Committee, the Southern Christian Leadership Conference and other groups during the sixties.

One day about six months ago I received a phone call from the sixth grade teacher at the public school on the corner where my son goes to school. The teacher invited me to come to the school the following week to talk to several classes of fifth and sixth graders. She explained that she would like for me to talk about careers, especially my own. She said the classes had recently taken several trips with the purpose of looking at various occupations. They had been to the bank to see people at work in the banking industry; they had visited an insurance company and some other businesses with the same thought in mind and she wondered if I would come and talk about my career.

At that time I was employed as copyeditor and proofreader of a newspaper.

After I hung up the phone, I wondered to myself whether she had meant for me to talk about my job at the newspaper. For in spite of the fact that I was employed at the paper, my vocation is liberation.

I knew that many of the teachers at the school knew of my involvement in the South with the sit-ins, and as an organizer with the Student Nonviolent Coordinating Committee and with the Southern Christian Leadership Conference, but I really was not sure which "career" she had in mind that she wanted me to talk about.

As I considered it, I realized that I could not talk about vocations if I talked about my job at the newspaper for I was only working there to make a living and with the knowledge that I *must,* before too long, find a way to make a living for myself and Sherri and Doug (my two children) and at the same time be about my real work. I felt terribly negative about the job. The truth is that having spent forty hours a week for three and one-half years on a job that interested me not at all, I was really unhappy.

Let me say more about that. I was miserable. First off, I was the sole support of our family because my former husband, the children's father, decided that he did not want to hold a job and he contributed nothing to our income. Since he was unemployed and in another state, the possibilities of legally forcing him to support the children were not there. Persuasion, having friends talk to him, etc. had failed utterly. So my salary was the sole income for our family and not by my choice.

One of my tasks at work was handling photographs belonging to the newspaper. I would constantly have come across my desk photos of black people riddled by bullets in the back or the back of the head by police; black children victims of starvation; students demonstrating for justice shot down dead in the streets by police of Latin American countries; during that time Fred Hampton and Mark Clark were killed. Angela was jailed. Two just men from the Sudan were executed. Pictures from Vietnam by the score came in showing the most horrendous crimes against the Vietnamese brothers and sisters and children. It was hard to reconcile the fact that I wasn't doing what I could do, small though it may have been, to improve things and add my weight against injustice. I would often look at a picture and emotion would well up and I would start the process of rationalizing. But I knew that if I did that over a period of time I would become desensitized and would become a person I did not want to be. We really are what we do—or don't do.

Sometime before, I had painfully come to the realization that working full time and taking care of the house and kids was all the work I could do. I had tried working with several groups that were doing things in the community and had found that I would either take on tasks that I could not accomplish or I would be overworked and find myself very tense, strung out and likely to scream at the children. I think that it is not revolutionary to raise children that feel neglected and that everything else is more important to their mother than having time to talk with them or help them with their homework or just enjoy them.

So after I would get home, fix dinner, do the dishes, spend some time with the kids and do a few household chores, I really didn't have any energy left, so I finally had to realize that and accept it.

Even so, a half hour at an appointed time each evening is not adequate for mothering small children. One of the things that was hardest to see was my children needing more of my time than I was able to give. My son overtly showed a reaction to lack of attention; he was very susceptible to the "class clown" syndrome. During a rare moment one day when I wasn't rushed (I had taken a day off from work) the house got too warm. I picked Doug up so he could see the temperature indicator on the thermostat and showed him how to turn it down. The intensity of his delight at having learned this skill made me realize how often it was that I passed up opportunities to show him things and just did them myself because I was usually pressed for time and it was often quicker just to do things myself. And such things are very important to a child's development in terms of his own concept of how well he handles the world. Anyway, this incident I give you as typical of the attitude we were in by my having to spend so much time on a job—I saw my children growing up and I knew no day would ever be relived and I was missing so much of their childhood—and they were missing so much of their childhood.

In addition, I had so little money, I could never pay all my expenses, not to speak of any extras ever. I knew that any person who worked 40 hours a week ought to be able to live comfortably. Those were the hardest years of my life (1969-71).

We are tempted to think that our experiences are only personal, but this is seldom true. Usually there are thousands of people who share a similar circumstance. There are great numbers of single women raising their children alone who haven't been fortunate enough to have secured a job which they find satisfying and who are caught in the circumstances of trying to make a living (and I don't mean a luxurious one) for themselves and their children and at the same time are seeing their children and themselves suffer emotionally. In addition it is quite devastating to have to (or to think you have to) work for your material living and invest major time and energy into tasks that you do not feel are really important to be done. A basic change will have to be instituted in our society to deal with adults and children in this circumstance without their having to go into starvation.

Then, on the job itself—it was one of those situations where being part of the right clique was most important. How well you did your job and how productive you were were not important when it came to raises and promotions. Your sex (being female was a disadvantage) and who you were "in" with counted much more, so therefore there were often incompetent people in supervisory positions who got there by gaining favor with the "right" people. Since I'm not good at apple polishing, I wasn't in the "in-groups" and this set of circumstances didn't help either.

All these things being true, I couldn't talk to the children about the adventures of journalism and be positive about working for a newspaper. I'd have been lying or I'd have brought them a negative thing or if I had tried to be positive, they were sure to have picked up the way I really felt about the whole thing.

I decided to talk about my real profession—being a freedom fighter. And as I got to thinking about it, I reflected that we often ask children what they're going to be when they grow up—a doctor, a teacher, fireman —even soldier. But the profession of freedom fighter is a legitimate profession. Not only is it legitimate, but it is vitally needed. When we are stimulating the aspirations of our youth and naming possible future vocations for them, such as doctor, teacher, policeman, etc., why don't we name freedom fighter?

Then I saw that I would have to explain in simple language what a freedom fighter is and what a freedom fighter does. (Isn't it a pity that we should have to explain that?) The only communities I can remember being in where it wouldn't have been necessary to explain to the children what freedom fighters are, were in Mississippi and various communities in the South where freedom workers from SNCC and SCLC were always around and the children soon learned what we were doing and what we were about. The other place was the Democratic Republic of Vietnam (North Vietnam) where almost everyone is a freedom fighter and where the children's whole education is geared toward becoming freedom fighters whether they are learning in primary grades or on the university level. If they are preparing to become a teacher, for example, they are given an orientation of becoming a teacher so that they can liberate people from ignorance and thus from anyone that would attempt to oppress them.

So I started getting really excited about the prospects of raising so important an alternative to the children. And when *Katallagete* approached me about writing an article on vocations I thought some people might have been looking for ways to present to their own children or to children they work with, the possibility of pursuing a vocation wherein they will work towards their own growth and freedom as well as towards the growth of others, and I hope that in some way this experience may be of benefit to some readers and some of their children who have been born into this beautiful but messed up world.

What follows is an outlined sketch of how the discussion went. It is a composite of the outline I took into class and some of the children's input. . . .

INTRODUCTION

We are going to talk about careers today. I would like to begin by asking you a question. Why are you in school?

Children: To learn

Yes. Now, for what purpose do we need to learn?

1. It's a natural thing to do. We can't help but learn. Like touching something hot teaches us something.

2. To be able to take care of ourselves. To be able to get a job. To be able to make money.

3. To do work that is important to us and/or to other people. Such as being a doctor to make people

well, being a teacher to teach children things they need to know, etc.

I am going to talk with you about a career or occupation where the person does something important to himself and to other people. We are going to talk about the freedom fighter. And those of you who will become freedom fighters when you get older and grow up will have to study very hard to prepare yourselves.

WHAT DOES A FREEDOM FIGHTER DO?

1. He (she) loves people (that includes oneself) and thinks people are the most important thing in the world. He is willing to work and if necessary die for people.

2. He thinks. A revolutionary will see or feel something wrong, some condition of injustice. He will not stop until he *understands* what is wrong and then he figures out how to make it right. He doesn't believe things just because someone says them; he thinks for himself. (We talked about some things that were unjust and about bad conditions in our own neighborhood. There were plenty—this is a hard-core ghetto area in Chicago.) I asked if they had magic wands and could make a change what change would they make. Among the changes were: "to make it so people (children and grownups) wouldn't fight all the time," "a new house for my family," "a bicycle," "a whole new outfit of clothes for my mother," "stop the war in Vietnam," "I'd make my family happy." I added enough good food for everyone in our community, houses that have no rats, roaches, leaking roofs, are warm in the wintertime and look nice, schools where all the children learn a lot and

are smart, etc. I explained the basic problem of blacks being poor and dependent because we own virtually no land and no natural resources. (Many were good freedom-fighter potential; they *understood* the problems first hand and many could articulate them.)

3. After the freedom fighter understands the problems and figures out how things can be set right, he must then *do* what is necessary to make things right. What are *some* of these things?

—He might write books, newspaper or magazine articles or leaflets to make other people understand what's wrong and how to make it right and what they must do if they want to make things right.

—He talks to people—door to door, holds meetings, and sometimes organizes big rallies.

—He may raise money.

—He teaches himself—he reads, and talks to people who know things he needs to know in order to learn.

—He organizes people to make change. He gets people into groups so that they can move together to do things that it takes many people to do.

—Sometimes he carries weapons and fights.

—Sometimes he is put in jail. Sometimes he is even killed.

—He does not stop until the change is made.

EXAMPLES

I used pictures and slides of freedom fighters from Vietnam, the southern African liberation forces (Mozambique, Angola, etc.) and from the United States (Freedom Riders, Selma Right-To-Vote campaign, etc.) where the freedom fighters fought without using guns and won battles over an opposition (police, sheriffs, etc.) who used guns.

There are children all over the world who are preparing to become freedom fighters. I showed pictures of schools in the liberated area of South Vietnam, children in FRELIMO (Liberation Front of Mozambique) schools, and mentioned that the future freedom fighters in the United States were among them, perhaps sitting right in this very classroom right now.

For Right Now

I said, if you think you want to be a freedom fighter when you grow up, you must study very hard. If you are stupid you can cause yourself and other people who trust and need you, to be hurt or even killed needlessly. Your real opposition will be educated. Many of them are rich and their parents spend a lot of money on their educations. They will be greedy and inhumane people, but you must not underestimate them. You can outmaneuver them and accomplish your objective because you will be on the side of truth and justice and they will not. But you must do your job with excellence.

A Final Word

If you were going to be greedy and selfish and exploit a group of people, and steal from them, one thing that would help you would be to find a way to keep especially young males from fighting you. One way to do that would be to get a large number of them on drugs. They'd stay all doped up and out of it or they'd be thinking about how they were going to steal from somebody (even from each other) so they could buy some more drugs. And they wouldn't be able to fight you. You could do anything in that community and the young men wouldn't even bother you and try to make you stop.

Now that's what's happening. And people on dope will try to tell you it's a hip thing. But that's because they don't understand the game that's being run on them. Our community is poor because somebody is stealing from us. And those people bring dope in to keep our young people from fighting them and they make a lot of money on selling dope besides. So if you want to be a freedom fighter, you must keep away from drugs because you must be strong and in good health.

Question and Answer Period followed.

You may wish to use this as a kind of guide or outline for discussion with an individual child or a group. Of course, do your own thing, making it as relevant to the children's own experiences as possible.

I would just like to add that in spite of the drugs and the crime and rip-off syndrome that many of the country's youth have gotten into and in spite of the fact that some have misunderstood the meaning of liberation and have thought it meant be insensitive to other people and plain uncouth, we do have great reason to be very proud of the country's and the world's youth with their widespread positions on the war in Indochina, violence, truth, love, ecology, etc.

Those of us twenty-five, thirty, and older must provide a framework for youth who want to be positive forces wherein they will be able to channel their energies into positive things (The armed forces and the gangs have an organized structure where youth can enter, and have certain basic needs provided while they carry out destruction, murder and crime). We must provide an ideological and material structure as efficient as the army for youth to work from in constructive action. We also must give enthusiastic encouragement to the oncoming generation of freedom fighters.

The End of the Affair

Robert Coles

Robert Coles is a psychiatrist who has written extensively
on the problems of children and poverty. His books include *Children of Crisis* (three volumes); *Still Hungry in
America* (with photography by Al Clayton); *Eric H. Erikson: the Growth of His Work;* and *Farewell to the South.*
He presently lives and works in Albuquerque, New Mexico.

Until my junior year in college I had no interest in
becoming a physician, and all during medical school I

had no desire to become a psychiatrist. If I were at Harvard today I would probably major in a field called History and Literature, but in the year 1950 I could only take an English course on the 19th century American novel, another one on contemporary drama, and a couple of history courses. Eventually I wrote a thesis on the work of Dr. William Carlos Williams—whose poems and essays I lived with and loved, and whose profession (he was a general practitioner) I eventually decided to pursue—at a very late date so far as the committees on admissions of various medical schools were concerned. Suddenly I had to take courses like biology and chemistry and physics, all of which bored me no end. I had trouble understanding lectures and I couldn't turn pages in books. But before long I had a solution for my loneliness and confusion and fear. I became a priggish snob. I turned on my class-mates with a vengeance. The trouble was not in my mind or in the sciences my mind was unprepared to absorb. The trouble, I decided, was in the students, many of whom wanted to be doctors at any price, doctors period. They studied hard and fought one another, fought the "curve," the grading curve which their professors obligingly set up for them. In the laboratory they were merciless with one another: I can recall the smiles when flasks were accidentally broken, and those grim faces peering at the scales as the "yields" were measured and scored.

To be blunt, a lot of the students were Jewish, so many that in some sections of the laboratory, where friends inevitably congregated, any Irish and Italians and Yankees around were distinctly noticeable—this at Harvard. For a while I wondered what had happened to me. I had no sociological eye, but I sensed a differ-

ence in all sorts of things between many of the Jewish
students and their classmates—dress, interests, manner
of speech; and I was rather annoyed, as I recall, when
my mind found itself unable to ignore and forget those
differences. Twenty years ago so-called Wasps were a
much larger majority in all the Ivy League schools.
There were a handful of Negroes and interestingly
enough, not too many Catholics. The number of Jews
was small but rising—and I suspect that development
was not completely unlike the one taking place now,
when the number of black students increases each year
at Harvard. In any event, the Jewish students in my
class—and for that matter, others who came from what
social scientists call "upwardly mobile" homes—weren't
as attracted to a course called "Proust, Joyce and
Mann" as to those courses that had to do with organic
chemistry or government or economics: and indeed just
as I was discovering much of that, a "team" of graduate students documented the same thing, all of which,
naturally, the local papers considered to be news.
Around that time I was obviously struggling with rather
ordinary decisions, the kind that college students always
have to make. I wasn't going through an "identity-
crisis," thank God. (In the early '50's, Erikson was just
formulating that kind of hang-up.) I wasn't even having
a "late adolescent adjustment reaction," as I gather
they were then called. If there were any psychiatrists
at Harvard I didn't know of them. (Now there are
many, and students flock to them.) If my parents gave
me any troubles, I didn't *think* about them as troubles,
or call them names, call them problems or complexes
or whatever. And if a friend had told me that I would
one day be a psychiatrist, I might have finally thought
about such a doctor—for my friend.

In my senior year I persisted with the new course I had set. I took more pre-medical courses; and though I primarily did so because Dr. Williams and his words and his ideas and his life meant so much to me, I also had other reasons in mind. I had to do something; or to put it differently, I didn't feel free to bide my time and make no decision about a career or a job or a profession until much later on. My parents were not putting any pressure on me, certainly none that was explicit, but they had their ideas and their values and I was more influenced by them at college than I knew. When I told them I might become a doctor they were surprised, not altogether happy, but very pleased. And when I saw how pleased they were, I realized that somehow I hadn't been forgetting my parents, after all. They had in fact been nearer to me than I could admit —even though I considered them reasonably agreeable, easy-going people, perfectly willing to leave me alone, even as I wanted to stay at college and away from them most of the time.

But they are a somewhat unusual and confusing pair, my mother and father, and I had best spell out why right away—because it is narratively sensible and appropriate to do so rather than psychologically sound. The odds that two people like them would ever meet and marry couldn't have been much lower, which occasionally must have made them anxious and certainly made me stop and wonder at various moments. My father was born in Yorkshire, England, of what I suppose could be humorously called "old Anglo-Jewish stock." That is to say, his family is descended from the Sephardic Jews who lived in Spain, and eventually had to leave there for countries like Holland and England.

My father was told by his grandfather that their descendents came to England several hundred years ago, were expelled, lived in Belgium and France, then came back to England in the late 18th century. It was he, my great-grandfather, who made the first break with that past. *His* father, my great-great-grandfather, was a rabbi, apparently a proud and powerful English Jew who wrote essays, poetry, and two volumes of philosophy. My great-grandfather was also supposed to be a rabbi, but said no, and became a lawyer, as did my grandfather. Something happened to those two, to my great-grandfather and my grandfather; something that didn't happen in the 19th century to many English Jews, but to some yes, and later to many more in America as well as England. I remember as a child hearing the whole business summarized by my mother: "Your father and your grandfather were brought up not to like a lot of things Jewish." I wanted to know if "things Jewish" meant Jews, and she hesitated—which I can vividly see in my mind right now—and felt compelled to talk and talk and talk: about the habits and idiosyncrasies that people the world over develop, and about the effect of persecution upon human beings, all of which meant to me that my father didn't like Jews and my mother was embarrassed to talk about the matter.

My mother had always liked Jews, among them my father. She comes from Iowa—Sioux City, Iowa. She is Episcopalian, the daughter of an Episcopal minister. Her grandfather was a farmer, and two of her father's brothers were farmers, very prosperous farmers who owned a lot of land and worked hard to make it productive. She met my father in Boston, where she was visiting two cousins, who had been sent East to college, to Wellesley College. Their mother was my mother's aunt, and their father a Yankee doctor who went to Iowa after graduation from medical school. My mother's cousins "fixed her up" with a blind date and he turned out to be my father, who had come to America so that he could study engineering at Massachusetts Institute of Technology. (At that time young English scientists often went to America or Germany for graduate education.)

My mother is a warm, emotional and very religious woman. She was brought up on the Bible, the Book of Common Prayer and the Apocrypha and she knows them all well. She has a mystical bent, never out of control, but always there. She makes a point of questioning "worldly" things—but at the same time has had no apparent trouble enjoying them. It was not hard for me as a teen-ager to find all her vague, pietistic talk a lot of chatter. I would bring home a good report card, and be told "fine"—but reminded about the sin of pride, and the dangers of "worldliness." My father, a worldly scientist, obviously found my mother's sly, opaque religious homilies rather charming—when they were not terribly frustrating and maddening. When Shakespeare was summoned to tell us that "there are more things in Heaven and earth . . . ," he would ask *what* things? When the Holy Ghost was mentioned as the court of last resort, he would ask, for the millionth time, what the Holy Ghost was, anyway. He was always good-natured, of course, or at worst only fretful; but he made his point for us, my younger brother and me, which is what I now know he wanted to do.

If my mother could be annoyingly evasive and devout and cloudy, my father could be stubbornly, narrowly perceptive. He saw what he saw clearly and deeply, and he spoke what he thought crisply and tersely; but there were whole worlds that he had no interest or desire to see, and they were not only religious or philosophical worlds: "I don't know about things like that," he'd say when my mother would talk about "grace" or a "redemptive moment." He always wanted to analyze: chemicals, which he did for a living and out of love; words, which in the form of etymological excursions was a hobby; and even people, whom he would call "basically" this or that. Some of the classifications and descriptions went like the following: "he's good stock gone bad"; or "he can't relax himself, and that's the way he'll always be"; or "he never had enough money when he was young, and he can't forget that even now, when he has as much as he'll ever need." Though my mother sensed things—some of them hard for anyone else to sense—she never tried very hard to put her feelings into thoughts, let alone words. It would be *disedifying*—to use one word she did use, all the time and with great emphasis. She meant that one ought to be happy if one has found something out, sensed it, come to know it. To go a step further and say it—well, that smacks of pride: others have to be let in on the secret, turned into an audience, a source of applause and approval.

Yet, she talked and got her points across, even as my father fell into long, weighty, speculative monologues about such intangibles—to us children, certainly —as war or poverty or racism and their causes. We sat and listened, and as I grew older I had more and more trouble making sense of his ideas—and of my mother's apparent willingness to accept those ideas rather uncritically. To my father "life" was and always would be tough, inscrutable and demanding. There were few "answers" that lasted very long, only new questions, which in turn demanded new efforts at comprehension. Mingled with that kind of stoic resignation was a stubborn political conservatism that became increasingly unappealing to me the more I appreciated it. Each person has to work, and make his way in the world. Anyone who really wants to struggle and save and plan and do things will achieve not joy or contentment or fulfillment —what do *those* words mean?—but a reasonable degree of "security," a bit of money, a job, a sense of achievement.

The point was not to get too philosophical, not to question things very much. Freud said that when you begin to ask about "the meaning of life" you are already sick. My father said as much a thousand times. He wanted no part of large-scale social or political criticism —Robert Taft was a great hero of his—but he did reserve the right to go on at length about and scorn people who don't work, who are lazy, who think in endless abstractions. To him it was all either simple or ineffable: man seeks after food and love and money and power, after concrete people and concrete things. That's the way it is, and has always been; so we ought not get too "muddled-up," too theoretical, too complicated about things. (Unless they are chemical things, which are beautifully tangible.) And above all we should always remember that problems don't go away; they just take new forms.

One problem that never went away from him was the one that had to do with what he called "Jewishness." He had not been brought up Jewish. His father felt English and not Jewish, and several years after the death of his first wife (my grandmother) he married a Scotswoman. In point of fact he did the second time

around what his children would do the first time around
—every one of them, three daughters and two sons. We
are all religious half-breeds, my English cousins and my
brother and me. Not to feel Jewish meant a strange as-
sortment of things. For my father it meant spending a
lot of time criticizing what he probably feared could
never successfully be denied. It meant thinking (and
saying to his young children) that Jews bring a lot of
trouble on themselves—at a time when the chief trouble
was rather obviously coming from Aryans in Berlin.
It meant saying—I now realize in awful moments of
shame and humiliation and helplessness—that maybe
the trouble was deserved, the suffering a consequence
of actual wrongdoing. Aren't a lot of Jews pushy and
aggressive and loud-mouthed and vulgar and too smart
and clever? Aren't a lot of them crooks? Aren't they
always figuring things out, looking for angles of one
sort or another? Aren't they clannish? And don't they
think too much, and make everything so damned complicated and abstract?

I don't mean to say that he poured things out like
that. I am condensing a life-time's remarks, and in that
sense I risk making my father a caricature of himself,
and of the familiar anti-Semitic Jew. (Psychiatrists risk
the same thing every day—often without apparent worry
—when they describe and summarize lives.) But from
time to time something like what I've described would
be said, and those were the times I looked to my mother
for a rebuttal. On occasion there would be one: "That
is not so," or more pointedly, "hush." But on one point
they both agreed: one should work hard and study and
learn. Yet, one should not take this life, or the mind,
or a particular century or idea or system of ideas too
seriously. To my mother the risk is idolatry; to my father

the risk is self-importance, the self-importance that a good chemist like himself—who loves his history books —knows to be absurd. And the Jews, the Jews have staked everything on man, on man's mind, and on this life, this world, this one great chance, this awful, unending challenge.

So, an issue like "Jewishness" became something else—a means of expressing all sorts of values and preferences: for tennis and squash and hockey to "balance" a lot of academic interests; for a certain casual, wry detachment that would prevent intellectual absorption from getting out of hand; for a blend of materialism and idealism whose "tone" or character or whatever could be distinguished as English and American, but not Jewish. And yet, all the while, the Jewish "problem" was there. During the Second World War my father's family, proud and even distinguished, feared for their lives. For a while our English cousins were going to be sent over, "in the event Hitler should cross over." But they weren't. My father told us they would all die together, if necessary. At around that time, the early '40's, I was growing up, and beginning to ask questions: we go to church with mother, but wouldn't Hitler see it differently, and wouldn't a lot of other people right here? Are we Jewish anyway, Protestant Jews, half-Jews, or Jews so long as someone, anyone, anywhere felt prompted to call us Jews? And what *did* our parents stand for? Father was a scientist; yet he worked for a big company whose purpose was to make money and (so the government charged and proved) cut down rather than thrive on competition. Mother talked about spiritual matters, and loved dreamy, wistful paintings—which cost plenty of money. They both wanted me to do well in school, but my father was afraid

I'd become too scholarly, "too brainy," hence a Jewish intellectual; and my mother feared I would forget the "more important things," which meant in a way, the mid-western anti-intellectualism that her other-worldly manner conceals.

Rather as a compromise, then, they both ruled out for me a career in business or law, or the pursuit of a Ph.D. Of course I could be or do anything I wanted, but the preferred things would be architecture, engineering, teaching; something that required work and dedication and thought, but not too much thought; and something a good distance away from the suspect and tainted "commercial" world. My father's brother was a surgeon, but that was an awful life—and he had died young from it: long hours, constant worry and terrible responsibilities. So, when I told my parents that I, too, might be a doctor, my father thought of his brother, and asked me what *kind,* before he said "fine"; and my mother said she was very surprised—because she thought I would eventually "study history and then teach it." She knew that I had taken great pains to learn about the history of her family and my father's; about the mid-west and about northern England; about the Old Testament prophets, whom she adored and my father denied (a little too insistently) knowing at all; about the origins of the early Christian church, and especially the life of St. Paul, who also had a few religious ambiguities to deal with. What she didn't know was that the whole thing was too much for me, the tension between my father's chemistry and his kind of resignation, not unlike the kind Kierkegaard described, and his affection for Robert Taft and his denied Jewishness on the one hand; and on the other hand the Holy Ghost and "faith and faith alone" my mother talked about so much, and her expensive, catholic, artistic tastes and her passion for Jeremiah and Isaiah.

My father said "fine" when I said "a pediatrician." The only other comment he had was, "you really do admire William Carlos Williams." He is quiet, one for under-statement, and not much given to wordy, psychological analysis. Long before I became interested in psychiatry—in fact when I was a first year medical student—my father made an unforgettable and typically brief remark after "looking through" (he would never admit to reading such things) a book by Karl Menninger (or was it Karen Horney?): "It's not new and much of it is painfully obvious. What poets and philosophers and ordinary peasants have known through the ages those psychiatric characters [that is him, pure him] take hundreds of pages to say in the worst possible way. Their language is disgraceful, and they don't have the least bit of imagination. All they want to do is pin labels on people and human affairs."

He had no interest in pursuing the matter, nor did I at the time—though I was struck with his candid impatience and annoyance, his willingness to say anything. Years later, under psychoanalysis, I would remember all that he said, but particularly the words "those psychiatric characters." And I would remember my mother's comments, too: "I read some of those books, and each time I feel it's the same person I'm meeting, a person who is standing on a mountain and chooses to kneel down and look at a leaf or a pebble." There are times when I cannot stomach the far-off mist and fog that my mother's lofty view always seems to include, but she does see life, and sees it as larger than words and formulas—political, psychological and all the rest.

In medical school I left them, and left a lot else. For the first time I was away from the whole, stuffy New England tradition that my parents, both outsiders, nevertheless much enjoyed. (In a way, I later realized, that tradition gave them a common meeting ground; its mixture of asceticism and sensuality, guilt and indulgence, idealism and practicality, religious faith and hard-headed, here-and-now concreteness offered two such strangers plenty of room.) Since I decided to attend Columbia's College of Physicians and Surgeons, I was also away from the old familiar schools I had attended and liked; and I was in New York City, which was near Paterson, New Jersey and Dr. Williams. When I went to look at Columbia I told the grey, gaunt, laconic biochemist who interviewed me that I wasn't sure I'd make it, but I wanted a chance to try. Then, as we talked more, I sensed a man I liked and could trust. I told him I really had grave doubts about whether I even wanted to be a doctor, if it turned out I could be one—that is, stay the whole course. He said he knew, he knew how I felt; and he felt I had a right to know, to find out whether in fact I would become a doctor, because eventually my mind might—as he put it, unforgettably—"find something half interesting here in medical school."

I never did make that discovery in those four hard, troublesome years. Repeatedly I thought I would leave; and on several occasions, when I was too frightened and confused to do anything but stay, the dean began to feel I had best leave. From the beginning I had no aptitude for dissecting the corpse or spotting things under the microscope, though I loved looking at the forms and colors the slides offered the eye. I could only hope that things would get better in the third and fourth years, when there were patients to be seen rather than pieces of tissue and microscopic slides. But in a way when I started examining patients things finally got so much better that I had as much trouble as before. Each new patient became someone for me to talk with and talk with and talk with—to the point that my laboratory work, blood tests and such which we had to do on all patients, was slow and I failed to "work up" my "cases" quickly enough. "The point is to make a diagnosis as quickly as possible and know how to get sick people better," I was told by my preceptor, as he was called. Then he added his punch-line: "You're not here to do psychiatry."

It was meant to be, it could only be, "the unkindest cut of all." For all its popularity with a certain segment of the lay public, psychiatry still earns little more than apathetic tolerance from many physicians, who "deep-down" suspect its value, even its integrity as a profession. Rather quickly in most medical schools a handful of students identify themselves as future psychiatrists, for which they receive a good deal of pity from others. Pity, of course, can include contempt, sorrow or sympathy; and in the mind of the "ordinary" medical student all those feelings are due any young man or woman who is ready to spend five years as a student and an intern in order to turn immediately around, forget just about the whole business, and spend the rest of his life talking with people about their dreams and their worries.

I was not one of them. As the doctor put it when he reprimanded me, I was not there "to do psychiatry." When I was asked by the dean what I did intend to "do" I answered "pediatrics" without any hesitation, and he immediately smiled back his approval. "We always need pediatricians," he added, and I could only admire his wisdom, a wisdom, incidentally, that I was coming to know rather too well because I was a "border-line" student. He would call me in to ask me how I was getting along, the answer to which he damn well knew. I would say that I wasn't doing too well; and he would say yes, that was true. Then he would tell me that I had done very well at college, at a good college, and now they were all unable to figure out why I couldn't do equally well at medical school. I would murmur something about my woeful literary and historical interests, and each time he would take that as a serious challenge: medicine requires culture; medicine requires a "whole man"; medicine requires a "broad knowledge of the humanities and the social sciences"; and finally, each doctor must be an "alert, informed citizen." I could not argue, only feel amused or at loose ends. But his brief lectures invariably had the effect he must have desired. I studied just harder enough to stay in school—and in the fourth year, at long last, I came to the clerkship in pediatrics.

For two days I was genuinely excited as a medical student. Though the children were sick, they were not the very sickest in Babies Hospital, and I found them a real delight to be with and talk with. I loved helping them, and loved getting to know their parents. I found my mind again its old self. I could remember things easily and go on to learn unrequired facts and figures. For the first time I went to the school's library. (I had to find out where it was.) I looked up this disease and that one. I read about the masters, the pediatricians who fought and beat diphtheria and whooping cough and scarlet fever, the pediatricians who spoke out against child labor, against sending ten year old boys and girls into mines or factories. And I re-read some of the essays of Dr. Williams, the ones that give a doctor's view of mothers and fathers who are brought together in an utterly special way by a child's illness.

And then it happened, a small, silly moment that nevertheless brought me up short, and in fact ended what I suppose was all along an illusion of mine. We had to draw blood from our patients, and my patient, George, aged two, required a "work-up," and from me a "veni-puncture." I had learned how to take blood from the arms of my adult patients, and I began to lift up George's small, thin arm when the nurse moved toward me, even as I myself realized there were no ample and ready veins in so young a child. "You'll have to use the neck," she quietly said, and for a second or two I must have thought she had lost her mind. I stared at her, and she stared back. Then she moved toward the child, to hold his head and body so that we both could be done with the job. She was a nice nurse, helpful and intuitive and attractive and well-liked by the children. She also was experienced enough and intelligent enough to know that medical students are often callow youths, even innocent children. She saw me as I will never be able to see myself, presumably frozen solid and mute. I can still recall her words: "You don't have to do it. The doctor will. It's hard and most of the students don't try. I just thought you would want to."

So I had won her over, even as I had persuaded myself: I was going to be a pediatrician, consequently I was on no ordinary "rotation." I would do anything, she had noticed, because at last I had found my home, my work, my interest. But now something was wrong with me. A good nurse, she had no time to wait and speculate. In a few seconds she relinquished her hold on George. And in a few seconds I was not longer transfixed. Gracefully she told George he had a reprieve, and a bit desperately I began to enjoy that reprieve with George. I played with him and made him laugh, and after a while, giggle and get a little overexcited. When the nurse came back I was glad to go. Both George and I needed to quiet down.

There is no point now in dwelling upon the repercussions of that incident, except to say that I dwelled on it for weeks and weeks. I suppose that eventually I might have learned to do veni-punctures on the necks of young children, and do a lot of other difficult things that often simply have to be done if suffering children are to recover from the serious and inscrutable diseases that still bring them to hospitals. (Today a pediatrics ward can resemble a geriatrics ward. Various antibiotics and vaccines have virtually eliminated—among middle-class families—a whole range of once dreaded illnesses. What remains, as with the old, are disorders of metabolism or of the bones and joints, or the various kinds of cancer). In fact I did go back there a few weeks later to do that veni-puncture, that quite ordinary procedure. But I had finally realized what I should have known all along, that I was not meant to work on children, to fix their bones or draw blood from them or analyze supplies of their urine or cut out their ailing organs or read their x-rays or in general devote my hands and head to the kind of relentless and stubborn and obstructive fight against death and pain and suffering that pediatricians unselfconsciously wage. Again, it wasn't the veni-puncture; it was a realization that the end of medical school was near, and my mind was still restless and bored and confused. Yet, I had no desire to return to Cambridge and study literature or history.

In a way I had come not only to respect physicians but envy them: somehow they could put a lot of inconsequential or trivial things aside and attend to very important business; somehow they could *do*—and not talk, talk, talk.

I had two very close friends while in medical school —one is now an internist in St. Louis, the other an ophthomologist in San Francisco—and in our last weeks as students both saw little hope for me but psychiatry. Actually I had done very poorly in the psychiatric clerkship at the New York State Psychiatric Institute of the Columbia-Presbyterian Medical Center. The patients were terribly lost and sad; and I could only laugh (as indeed they did, on occasion) at my feeble efforts to reach them. Our teachers were awful. I couldn't understand what they were talking about. They seemed anxious to prove they were scientists. They used long words, and never really explained them satisfactorily. My particular preceptor was an arrogant, vain, dogmatic, parochial man—and if other doctors or indeed other people are like that, the subject matter made those personal characteristics hard to ignore or forget. Nor could we forget the cheap slogans and handy clichés that he pushed at us. One in particular became endlessly repeated by virtually everyone in the class: "It doesn't make any difference whether you do it while hanging from a chandelier, so long as the penis is in the vagina. Remember, P in V." Now we were not there to help Joseph Heller write *Catch-22*. We were supposedly there to hear a sensitive, thoughtful psychiatrist, a professor of psychiatry, teach us something called "psychosexuality." And we learned our lesson: whether we were in the cafeteria, on the wards, leaving a sexy movie, or in a chorus scene of our class play, the slogan "P in V" came to mind, along with a few other emphatic expressions we had picked up. "It's oedipal, it's oedipal"; or "always look for the resistance"; and "remember, instincts and defenses against instincts, instincts and defenses against instincts, that's what goes on in the mind."

My resistances (and today I would dare say, my better instincts rather than my defenses) caused me to fall noticeably asleep twice during our "small-group" lectures; and I received a C— for the course, as low as one could go without flunking—and incidentally, the lowest grade I ever received in any clinical subject. All of which is to say that when my friends mentioned psychiatry as a career for me they were not commenting on an interest of mine, but responding to my confusions with their own exasperation. It was as if they saw me going to Hell, and wanted to warn me, warn me by saying the word that describes Hell.

The confusion persisted during internship. I left New York for Chicago, on the assumption that yet another city would help out. I chose the University of Chicago Clinics, a first-rate hospital which allowed interns to rotate through several fields (medicine, surgery, obstetrics and gynecology, pediatrics) rather than concentrate on one; and a hospital which was right in the middle of a university setting, as Columbia's medical school was not. I could always audit an English course or run to the public lectures that are held in such a university—or so I thought.

That year was a nightmare for all of us interns. As internships go, it was a very tough one. We could never leave the hospital unless we were willing to sign over responsibilities to another doctor. That is, there were no days off, time that was by right ours. We were expected to do an enormous amount of laboratory work, blood and urine analyses that in many other hospitals either technicians or medical students did. And of course for the first time *we* were the doctors.

I worked and worked and forgot everything except the next job, the next patient to be worked up, the next operation. The four months on surgery nearly broke me physically, though to my surprise I found the work rather appealing. The hardest month was the one spent on chest surgery. The surgeon I worked with was an old-timer, a work-horse, a crusty, fussy man whose warmth was never obvious and perhaps believable only to his patients. During that month I stopped smoking forever. I seriously considered quitting the internship. I never slept more than three or four hours at a time. I became thinner than thin. I pronounced ten victims of lung cancer dead. I became particularly attached to two others—yes, middle-aged "maternal" women who were a contrast with the men we mostly saw then. (Now, as more women smoke longer, more women develop lung cancer.) And finally, I almost decided to take a residency in chest surgery, to specialize in cardiovascular surgery, which was in its infancy then.

The hard work, the dramatic struggle against great odds, the chance to help build and develop a profession rather than join one already established, the sense of immediate contact with the very essence of the body's life, the heart and lungs—I suppose all that had something to do with my interest. In Gay Allen's biography of William James I recently came across the following: "My first impressions are that there is much humbug therein, and that, with the exception of surgery, in which something positive is sometimes accomplished, a

doctor does more by the moral effect of his presence on
the patient and family, than by anything else." Now, a
century later, I fear many students must still share
James' viewpoint. One of our teachers at Columbia told
us that "most of your practice will essentially be psychosomatic, and how you talk with the patient will
probably matter more than what you do." Certainly a
shift of some kind has taken place when "moral effect"
is dropped and a term like "psychosomatic" appears.
But how significant a shift is it, and even more important, how valuable a shift?

In the last few months of that internship I could
easily have qualified as one of the exceedingly troubled
and tired and cranky people William James describes
so beautifully. I was even beginning to have a "religious
crisis" of the kind he documented so extensively. I
doubted everything, particularly the value of the five
years of training I was just completing. I had no idea
what I would do next, took to staring at the sky and the
stars and the trees perhaps a little longer than usual—
and, of course, a little longer than is the custom of
psychiatrists, who set the standards in such matters and
claim the right to decide what is "normal" and what is
"excessive"; that is, on the way to being "abnormal." I
recall reading some of Thomas Merton's poems and
essays, and for a week I went to the town of Trappist,
Kentucky, Abbey of Gethsemani, not to be a monk, but
for a period of "contemplation," which I had heard was
permitted visitors, with no questions asked. At that time
I also was very much a student of Albert Schweitzer's
writings. I made inquiries about working in his hospital
at Lambarene, and other inquiries about hospitals in
India. I thought of going back to Harvard, to study
English or comparative literature at its Graduate School.

And finally, most tempting of all, I began to look at maps and speculate on which countries I would like to visit if I took a year or two off.

Eventually the possibility of work at Dr. Schweitzer's hospital became a probability. One of his closest aides, also a doctor, said yes, tentatively. The next step was up to me. When could I come, he asked. Well, when could I? But suddenly I heard my friends talking about the Army, about the "doctor's draft law" that sooner or later would get us all for two years. And suddenly I realized (in the fifties, when most students were automatically deferred until they were twenty-six, then considered ineligible for military service) that I had lost more freedom than even I, full of self-pity, had imagined. To five wasted years, I would have to add the two additional years that every single doctor must give to the armed forces. I could not go to Africa or Asia or around the world or indeed anyplace without checking in with my draft board and with some representative of the Defense Department, which had been waiting all along for me since the first day I entered medical school, thereby submitting myself to a special law meant to guarantee that soldiers and sailors are supplied with plenty of doctors.

That seemed more than I could take—two years on some Army base in, say, Alaska. Yes, the imprisonment could be delayed, but only if a further commitment were made. In other words to be deferred again until I finish my training I would have to become a physician who intends to specialize in surgery or pediatrics or radiology. But a resident in what? In the middle of that year of internship, in the middle of the period devoted to surgery, I had thought: maybe that, maybe surgery, maybe five or so years of cutting and sewing up, even though I could do neither well. Now it was the end of the year, and I was exhausted and frustrated and confused—and no longer interested in surgery or anything else.

Around that time Paul Tillich came to the University of Chicago to give a series of lectures; and at the same time several prominent psychiatrists (I had never heard of them, but they were characterized as "well-known") arrived to speak to the medical school faculty. I listened to Tillich with great interest, and noticed that he devoted a lot of his time to issues like "guilt" and "shame" and the relationship between psychotherapy and religious introspection. And quite by accident the psychiatrists were around, at the hospital, ready to discuss those same matters. Tillich drew large crowds, but as hospital conferences go, so did the doctors. They were, of course, different crowds; Tillich attracted the general public and people from all over the university; the doctors attracted an unusually large number of fellow-doctors and medical students. The year was 1955, and I can still hear the remark of the internist who sat next to me. I had worked with him for a month (he specialized in metabolic diseases) and we had become friends. At the end of the psychiatric meeting he turned to me and spoke: "Not bad. A lot of them are hard to follow, but they were pretty good. I guess we need them. They remind you of a lot of things you should know anyway if you're going to be a good doctor; but I suppose you have to be reminded."

There was more; we had a long conversation as we walked back to his laboratory. Later that day in the bookstore I picked up a book called "A General Introduction to Psychoanalysis" by Sigmund Freud, whom I knew about but had never read. A few days later I asked a friend of mine, another intern who planned to be a psychiatrist, what else he recommended. He suggested Erik Erikson's *Childhood and Society,* which I bought and read and found quite compelling.

So, I went back to my friend, who worked with those obscure metabolic diseases, and asked him whether he would think me a complete fool if I took a year's residency in psychiatry—perhaps concentrating in the field of "psychosomatic medicine," then a widely used term to describe what was really a way of looking at a number of diseases, like ulcers, asthma or colitis. "No," he said, "it might be a damn good thing to do."

I decided he was right, and set about applying to hospitals, not mental hospitals, but general hospitals which offered a psychiatric residency. I wanted to learn psychiatry, but I also wanted—strangely in view of the five years struggle that was then ending—to remain a practicing physician. Within weeks the letters of inquiry were answered by letters with application forms, which were filled out and returned. Next I had to be interviewed, and inevitably, asked *why* I wanted to be a psychiatrist, and *when* I decided to be one, and *what kind* of psychiatry interested me. In Chicago and New York I was asked so many questions I almost gave up applying. I was trying to assert a kind of new and tentative, but I thought serious, interest; and they were trying to find out whether something, somewhere in my past accounted for that interest. Had I ever thought of therapy? No. Had I ever thought of analysis? No. Had I ever worried about my mind, felt close to a breakdown? No—but, yes, I've had my moods. I've felt low and I've felt good. I mean—well, I've never had any

problems that I considered serious, though I've had my
doubts and misgivings about things. About things? About
what things? Well, as I said, I've not quite known what
to do, which kind of medicine to practice, if any at all.
And lately, yes lately, I have been thinking about psychiatry, and I've read some books. Books? Which
books? Well . . . What did I think of them? Well . . .

And twice I was put through something I later discovered was a "stress interview," done to see how strong
or fragile my "defenses" are. Why, why, why—the
questions flew across the room. What would I do if . . . ?
What would I do if . . . ? What was my mother *really*
like, and my father? How come I was so "attached" to
Dr. Williams, and to "literary books"? (Yes, that was
the term.) I felt frightened and angry—and really rather
appalled, though I was determined to be as quiet and
controlled as possible. In one of the interviews I was
called a "snob." I was told I was "overoccupied with
religious thoughts." I was informed that my politeness
was all veneer, a denial of hostility, a "reaction-formation." When I asked what a "reaction-formation" was,
that request was interpreted—as further evidence of my
hostility. What would I do, bellowed the interrogator,
when I was face-to-face with *sick* people, *hostile* people,
psychotics—who would "bombard" me (another hard-
to-forget word) with—well, he called it the "negative
transference." I recall wondering what *that* was—and
thinking it couldn't be anything more rude or cheap or
vulgar or foolish than what I was experiencing right at
that moment. And in a way I knew what both of those
characters, those "psychiatric characters," were up to. I
didn't formulate their behavior as a "stress interview." I
simply decided that they were being harsh and nasty
and unnecessarily prying and presumptuous and really,

far less clever or original than they thought. (Inquisitions have plagued men for centuries.)

But I was shaken by the experience; and rather curiously, I was "hooked" by it, too. I wanted to know what those doctors thought they could possibly be accomplishing. They seemed quick, intelligent, sensitive—for all their almost automatic discourtesy and their episodic brutishness. After I had left their offices I began to feel like a good school-boy again. The world is made of teachers and students, I reminded myself. Those psychiatrists were teachers, and I was a supplicant, a would-be student. They *had* to question me like that. They had to *make sure*. Anyway, the good student obeys, and particularly as he gets older the good student enjoys his uncritical, slavish obedience, because he will soon be through—and ready to be a teacher himself. I knew the awkward humiliating moments would soon end. Youth no longer seemed quite so far from authoritative adulthood. And doesn't compliance become a habit after a while, one so ingrained that—perhaps only a psychiatrist can do something to change things!

I guess my "defenses" weren't so bad. I guess I knew how to "rationalize" like a trooper, and do a bit of "sublimating," too. I was accepted wherever I applied. I chose—back in Boston—a very fine general hospital, with a small psychiatric service. I had in mind a year on that service, and then perhaps a try at medicine or even—once again—pediatrics, both of which I could also study at that hospital. My friends in Chicago and my parents in Boston were, to say the least, surprised and disappointed, each for different reasons. To my father psychiatry was hocus-pocus, and a "habit of self-contemplation" as he put it, a waste of time. To my mother life is by nature full of problems, and it is those problems that enable what grandeur, what destiny man finds in his brief stay here. She finds psychiatrists naive and a bit vain, a bit self-centered, rather a contrast to what *they* consider themselves: guardedly pessimistic and very hard-working. She didn't get too worked up about my decision, but she did let me know what she thought: there is something presumptuous about the way psychiatrists write and talk and look at the world; they don't very often mention the rights of their patients —to a degree of privacy, to the self-respect that comes from a person's own eventual triumph over an admittedly long and arduous psychological enemy; and worst of all, like many social scientists and political reformers, psychiatrists tend toward the simple-minded assumption that man can somehow shed himself of life's ironies, ambiguities and inevitable disappointments. "They are all too clear-cut in their descriptions," I remember her saying when I mentioned the psychiatrists I had met— whose ranks I then proposed to join. Then she went on, briefly but with unusual sharpness, and even some bitterness: "They like to put everything into their theories —the world, the devil and the flesh. They think they know more than they do, and they don't like hearing others, who know other things, things I'm afraid they never even think about."

Until I told them my decision, I never knew how much she and my father knew about Freud's thinking, or Jung's, or Erich Fromm's. And as I look back now, I realize that their disapproval, mildly and cautiously stated, as always thoroughly understated, meant a lot to me. At last, at last, I had decided to do something that they really didn't much like; *both* of them. For once, in fact, they were ideologically united. That is, for once I could disagree with the two of them. I did

not have to take sides. They were philosophically together—and I felt rather delighted with myself. Their
combined opposition ironically meant that I had something going for me.

And in that psychiatric residency, which eventually
was to last not one but four years, I also learned how
strong—or strong-minded—psychiatrists can be. Indeed, everything is grist for the mill: wars, riots, illnesses
of all sorts. Surgeons sublimate "aggression" or "sad-
ism." Lawyers are "obsessive" and struggling with
"super-ego problems." And what do doctors *really* want
to heal or cure? It all seems rather funny to me now,
but it wasn't very funny a short decade ago, when I was
finishing up my training: bewildered, half-indoctrinated,
very much afraid to say anything critical about a profession that for all its deficiencies still offers its members
a chance to work with troubled people—who, God
knows, need whatever friendliness and concern and intelligence they can find in other human beings.

Yet, it took me all too long to realize that, to fix in
my mind what the practice of psychotherapy actually
is: two people coming to terms with one another, getting
to know one another, learning from one another, meeting one another over an issue or issues in one particular
life; but eventually—in dozens of subtle and implied
and often unspoken ways—sharing feelings about life in
general. Instead, for more months than I care to admit,
for years in fact, I became all taken up with quite another way of seeing things, of thinking and getting
along with people.

Almost from day one of training we learned to *type*
people, to hear their "complaints" (the outpourings of
their minds and hearts were reduced to that, to the
word "complaint" or the word "problem") and then to

call them something. I can remember the first patient I
met, a quiet, sad lady who became very discouraged
after her first child was born. She came into the hospital
because she feared for her life and the baby's life. "If
I don't feel better, how can I take care of him, and of
myself?" she asked me over and over again. I had no
answer to that. I didn't dare to tell her that indeed she
couldn't, as she feared, take care of herself or her child
if she continued to feel low in spirits. But I knew what
to do, all right. I knew how to change the tack of the
conversation. I knew how to probe. That's what we
were taught, right off: to probe, to find out, to go back
in time, to learn antecedent events or causes, to take
note of "associative" thoughts and fantasies as the patient talks, to learn what is *really* being said, in contrast
to what the patient *thinks* he or she is saying.

So, I probed. She wanted to know how she would
be able to take care of herself and her new-born son,
and I wanted to know about her family and her childhood and her habits and tastes and preferences—in
general, about *her*. All well and good, until my supervisor asked me what caused the "depression," what
"specifically" had happened to make her "sick." I
hadn't thought of her as sick, and it had never occurred
to me that moods responded so precisely to life's experiences and circumstances. "Let's turn the coin over"
he kept on saying, every time I reported on a conversation, "let's uncover the real meaning."

Slowly I was flipping coins left and right as I listened
to that woman and others like her, people whom I
learned to call "phobics" and "hysterics" and "psychotics," people whom I learned to diagnose more
quickly, more correctly, more authoritatively. They
came anxious, scared, worried, downcast, sometimes in

a world all their own, with sounds and sights hard for
an outsider to understand; and I became more and more
the self-confident listener, who knew what to ask and
how to answer, who knew how to turn back time, and
turn around remarks, and turn over coins, on the spot
as well as later with a supervisor. This means that. That
is a disguise for this. He is defending against—well,
there are dozens of things that require a "defense." On
it went. I learned a whole new language and never once
really stopped to smile, and recognize how comic some
of the words and phrases are. Nor were any of us residents in a mood to relax about the whole thing, to be
amused at the way psychiatrists look upon the world.
Quite the contrary, when we weren't analyzing our
patients we practiced on one another—and I must emphasize at this point that in doing so we were following
the obvious example of older people in the field, colleagues, men who every day in front of us chose to talk
about anyone, whether a figure in public life or a character in a movie or a play or a novel, as if each of them
were a psychiatric patient. I am embarrassed now to
think about the vulgarity and absurdity of it all; but it
did happen, and it continues to happen—I know that
for sure. Did you know that Kafka was a paranoid
schizophrenic, and Conrad a latent homosexual? Did
you know that Hemingway was "defending" himself
against his "passivity" (and a lot of other things) or
that the "sexuality" that writers like Norman Mailer
and Henry Miller press upon their readers masks other
things: fears and inhibitions, suppressed puritanism,
even a touch of insanity? I am not indulging in caricature now; rather it is understatement. To this day, at
important international psychoanalytic meetings I hear
social and political anti-Semitism tied up with "castration

anxiety" and wars "explained" by the simple-minded resort to abstractions like "instinctual aggression." And in the 1960's the journals continue to offer psychiatric and psychoanalytic "studies" that show how hung-up all those writers and artists were, not to mention the characters written about in dozens of novels or portrayed on all sorts of canvases.

But that nonsense needs no criticism here by me. What I have to live with is my own personal willingness to inflict on myself and those around me a very similar kind of narrow, reductionist thinking—that, above all, fails to appreciate the essence of each individual, which is not the presence of all those "conflicts" (who, exactly who, is without them?) but the use they are put to. My inclination now is to laugh at all those incidents, all the observations and interpretations that flew across supper tables or hospital corridors or conference rooms—directed not only at the vulnerable patients but ourselves, more vulnerable than we ever realized, more desperate and frightened, too. What else but nervous fear leads to frivolous, condescending, arrogant name-calling? You are late? Why? You avoid fish, or don't like asparagus or actively shun tangerines? Why? That necktie, what prompted you to buy it, to wear it, to wear it today? And of all clues and signs the most tell-tale is the automobile, which represents something called your "body-image." I badly needed a car in early 1957, but I waited and waited while I took my proper soundings. There were a number of "factors" to consider. The car's color made a difference, and its shape; and it mattered if I bought a convertible—which can literally stand for mixed or ambiguous sexual appetites. Long sports cars were "phallic symbols." A black car indicated a "possible depression." Red could mean something sexual, or something aggressive, or something exhibitionistic. I tell you again, it seems only funny now, but we were grown men and women, entrusted with the care of other grown men and women, and we thought like that—and so did our aging, incredibly watchful and strict supervisors, some of whom, I believe, might make Cotton Mather appear to be a rather relaxed and humorous man, after all.

I owe to my mother the first realization that puritanism had found so large and comfortable a home in 20th century psychoanalytic psychiatry. I invited several other psychiatric residents to my home, and my parents happened to stop by. Someone said something, and that was interpreted. Someone dropped something, and that was interpreted. Someone forgot something, and that was interpreted. And so it went. As my parents prepared to leave, rather quickly I noticed, my mother took me aside.

"What is the point to all that self-consciousness? Why do you all *behave* that way? It is so silly; and so boring, I have to add."

If she was angry, so was I. I felt talked to—like a child. That last "I have to add" was rather familiar, a mannered expression she used when she felt both annoyed and in a condescending frame of mind. We quickly said good-bye, and I returned to my friends, one of whom promptly remarked that I seemed to get along better with my father than my mother.

At this point *I* have to add that, apart from my mother and her comment, which I did not easily get out of my thoughts, there were rising currents of dissatisfaction in me—so that in my second year of residency I was beginning to look around, to look for a way out. For days at a stretch things would go along smoothly: symptoms were matched with diagnostic labels; motivations were exposed; "relationships" were analyzed; some patients felt better and others grew worse; supervisors listened and said yes or maybe or no; and I drifted along, looking toward a day when I would be completely trained, certified, free to practice and practice and practice—at long last a member of a profession. But suddenly I would begin to have my doubts. I would have finished an hour with a particularly difficult patient and my mind would insist on wondering. Why do some people become "sick" while others from equally troublesome backgrounds stay reasonably well? What makes patients better, the "correct" and well-timed interpretations I offer them, or something else going on between them and me? What about the millions of people on this planet who have never heard of psychiatry, or would never think of seeing a psychiatrist, or never be able to afford one? Do they simply make do, try to manage the best they can, against serious odds? Or do they know things about survival, endurance, courage, growth, strength that make people like me seem arrogant and narrow-minded. "They manage, they manage," one of my supervisors put it when I tactfully asked *him* that question—but then I wondered how he knew. All his patients paid him thirty dollars an hour, (then—they pay fifty and up now) and the ones I presented to him, the "ward patients," were invariably, in his words, "very hard to treat, very hard." They had, it seems, "character disorders." At that time I never thought to ask him about his private patients and *their* "character disorders." But a year later I did, and to his credit he was utterly, bluntly, disarmingly honest: "Yes, I see a number of them, with severe character disorders. But they're motivated. They come regularly and they're willing to pay."

By that time I was getting interested in patients who are often sly and irregular in all sorts of ways—and poor, so unable to pay for "help," as we used to put it so often. ("Boy, is he sick! Boy, does he need help!") I volunteered to work in one hospital's "alcoholic clinic," and I became interested in and eventually attached to a clinic that offered medical and psychiatric assistance to delinquent youths. I suppose the skid-row drunks often had a sense of humor, a sense of philosophical detachment, that I sorely missed. They were incurable and unenviable, but they could laugh and ask the most outrageous and often refreshing questions. I was told it was all part of their "infantile behavior," their "pre-oedipal personality structure," their "primitive orality." All of which goes for delinquents, too—many of whom I also found bright, warm, affectionate, witty, in their own way honorable, and to one another, intensely loyal. I was told they were "border-line," or they were "psychopaths" in the making, or "sociopaths."

But what did I know about their lives, those terribly drunk men or those incredibly clever and lonely and brash youths, all of whom had stories to tell that didn't suit my (by now thoroughly memorized) list of questions? I recall the moment when one delinquent asked me whether I had ever seen his neighborhood, his "turf." I said no, and tried to get him back to himself, to his "problems," to the reason he had stolen a car and assaulted a store-keeper, and dropped out of school. Surely there *was* a reason, a psychological conflict, a "psychodynamic" explanation. And surely that youth's street—including the houses on it, the alleys that leave it, the people who walk it and stand on it and stare at it day after day—cannot have much to do with his state of *mind*.

Believe it or not—the year was 1957—I talked with that young man for months and never really gave his race much attention. I wanted to know about his mother and the way she treated him, about his father and his behavior, about all those brothers and sisters. The father, I discovered, was a step-father, and he was not always around. The mother and son were thus thrown close together, or so it seemed. The "oedipal situation," as my supervisor kept on calling it, was thereby "heightened," and the result was "acting-out": the "boy" (as that same supervisor called him, perhaps revealing a bit of his own "oedipal situation") felt himself threatened by his mother's presence, his father's disappearance, his stepfather's absence—and without adequate "defenses," he took to delinquency, to a symbolic if illegal expression of his unconscious fantasies and conflicts. In my supervisor's brilliant formulation: "The car, you see, stood for his sexuality, his forbidden sexuality. His mother tempted him, he felt anxious and guilty, and so he *did* something—which expressed what was troubling him."

I remember having the naive thought that it was the car, the *car* that "tempted" him—as indeed cars tempt a lot of us. I remember thinking that a lot of young men in that neighborhood must be tempted by cars— even as their "peers" (as the social workers put it) in the suburbs ride in and own those tempting cars. And I remember thinking, for only a flash, that Lawrence was a *Negro*—and that his family was *poor,* very poor, and that they had recently come *North*. Well, there are, it is true, those "socio-cultural factors." But they are not really the "deep" problems, the "unconscious" problems, and so they are none of my business, or so I told myself, because so I was told to tell myself.

Again, I wish what I have been writing here were a caricature, or merely half-serious. I wish I were exaggerating or taking things out of context. In fact, I am—to use a word—suppressing all too much. "Remember, you're selling time; you're in the business of selling time," a fiftyish professor of psychiatry told us in one of those "case-history" seminars. He was "accredited" by every psychiatric and psychoanalytic organization. He was always talking, about techniques—the technique of ending an hour, or beginning one, or doing this and that. He was a vulgar man, in many respects a stupid man, though I didn't dare think so then, at least for more than a second. Anyway, in view of all the tyranny this century continues to witness, I suppose it is self-pitying and petty for someone like me to insist upon mentioning the mindless, insulting manner in which certain teachers turn young doctors, twentyish students, into willing compliant followers—who can, like their leaders, turn on the outsider and excuse anything in the insider. (The critic has "resistance," is "neurotic," needs "treatment"; and the teacher who others might consider narrow-minded and a little cheap is in fact honest and blunt—willing to say outright what everyone else keeps buried, as a result, naturally, of their "reaction-formations" and "denials.")

Toward the end of my training I enrolled in a seminar at Harvard given by Paul Tillich—perhaps because freedom seemed nearer and I could risk an encounter with his intelligence, his compassion, his grace, his real dignity as a person and a thinker: in sum, his healing presence. I began also to realize that there would always be a certain tension in me, not the kind psychiatrists talk about, but the kind Tillich described, calling upon St. Paul and before him the prophets of Israel: a tension between a belief in the letter and a search for the spirit; between a search for facts and an ear for speculations; between an interest in history, in its bulky and coercive weight, and a desire to recognize the possibilities that come with each ("existential") moment; between a recognition of the "inner" life of the mind and an awareness of the power that the "outer" life of the world exerts; between a wish for analysis and a longing for action; between the hunger for abstract explanations and interpretations on the one hand and the need to confront emotions, all sorts of troublesome or liberating (redemptive, if you will) emotions—and experiences and events and happenings, whatever.

In a curious and ironic way I was to find a certain kind of intellectual liberation in Mississippi, in the United States Air Force. There I could practice on my own and learn the value of my profession by seeing its tenets (the best of them, learned at great sacrifice and cost by Freud) come alive in concrete situations— which I was under no forced and arbitrary constraint to formulate. In the South I could also read more and more widely, read not only psychiatric and psychoanalytic textbooks, but those sane, literate and civilized psychiatric writers who truly follow Freud, each in different and not necessarily harmonious ways: Erik Erikson, Anna Freud, Frieda Fromm-Reichmann, Allen Wheelis, Harold Searles, Charles Rycroft, D. W. Winnicott—men and women who think clearly, who know how to write a straight sentence, who admit to honest uncertainty and bewilderment, who admit to and respect and even take comfort from life's ironies; and finally men and women who don't drown their doubts and worries in a muddied, turbid river of jargon.

In a sense I suppose that by the time I went South, a fully trained psychiatrist, I had already begun to right my balance; yes, to draw upon the common-sense my parents had fought to win for themselves. Just recently, as I was putting all this down, my mother asked me whether I had "consulted the Concordance" to find a title for a book I recently wrote—to which my father asked: "What will he find there?" They get along rather well, with ups and downs, of course. My mother's Bible, her guarded streak of mysticism, her mixture of romantic optimism and Calvinist pessimism, are all balanced by my father's what's and why's, his interest in facts, reasons, and explanations. They need one another, not in the debased, contemporary psychiatric sense of the word "need"—apparently profound but actually rather superficial—but in the sense of need that Henry James would understand: they have different sensibilities, different views of the world, and they become larger persons because they have one another to respect and acknowledge. Were my father's views like my mother's, I fear they both would have long ago floated away, or become hopelessly lost in some pleasant but unreal world of their own, perhaps one like the Aran Islands—where stubborn, unrelenting faith clashes against grim odds in a highly dramatic, almost apocalyptic (and uncommon, unrepresentative) fashion. Were my mother more like my father, I fear things would get dull. They would be far more cranky and limited people than they are. So it was a bit of balance I regret to say we lacked in those years of psychiatric training, a balance I feel the profession as a whole still very much needs, a balance I am mighty proud and glad I could somehow find—of all ironic places, in my childhood. Maybe it is a balance other professions also fail to offer young people who want to enter them.

In the South I went on to other interests, which I have chronicled elsewhere (in the three volumes of *Children of Crisis*). But before I could do so, stay South rather than return North to a world of labels and clichés, I had to immerse myself in novels and essays: in Agee and Orwell, in Flannery O'Connor and Georges Bernanos, in Simone Weil and Faulkner and Ralph Ellison, and later in Walker Percy's philosophical writings as well as *The Moviegoer* and *The Last Gentleman*. (In certain ways Dr. Percy keeps on reminding me of Dr. William Carlos Williams.) And I had to stop saying to myself: how wonderful that *they,* too, should have a glimmer of what *we* in the hospital know. In other words, I had to retreat, lose faith in all sorts of arrogant convictions, answers and formulas. Since *The God That Failed* has already been written, I do not propose the novitiate in psychiatry as anything more than a footnote to that volume. But the analogy does hold, as Erik Erikson implied when he wrote of "punitive orthodoxy" in psychoanalysis, and as Robert Lifton suggested when he had the courage and candor to compare certain aspects of psychiatric and psychoanalytic training with the "thought reform," the "totalism" that Russian and Chinese communists press upon their all too vulnerable—and ultimately willing—recruits.

We are victims of what bores us and outrages us; and sometimes victims become to weak to resist. I write all this to confess an early indifference and boredom that turned to outrage—later it seems, and not without a period of surrender. I write now because I think at last the affair is really over, the uncritical submission, the sense that anything is possible, given just a year more of knowledge and training, but also the later bitterness and regret. I write glad that I can do what I do, help out as a psychiatrist when it is possible to help out; and sad that there are failures—failures of "technique," or "transference," of the patient's "characterological structure," and most of all failures because of what takes place between men and other men, or women and other women, or men and women, some of them called "patients" and some of them called "doctors." And I write nervously, too—perhaps like a girl from a country town whose parents will soon find her out, visit her in New York or Los Angeles and find her a waitress in a Playboy Club. Why write all this? Why write about me, me, me? Why talk so much about my parents? Who cares? Why should I presume that others will care? Why *ought* they care? Haven't we enough self-serving egoists around—ready always to filter the entire world through their thoroughly limited and subjective and sometimes crazy senses? Or more pompously: what general "relevance," what "larger significance" does this story have, if any?

I cannot answer all those questions. But from time to time I do talk with college students and medical students and young psychiatrists-in-training; and from time to time I attend staff conferences, clinical conferences, psychiatric and psychoanalytic conventions; and when I feel particularly down and out I still read the journals, and as it were immerse myself in my mood. The faces of the students—not to mention the patients —continue to be full of hope and wonder and confusion and hunger and not a little fear. The older psychiatrists still squabble and quibble. The journals are, as I have indicated, as my father would say, "a bloody bore." There are, of course, good moments—"moments of grace," my mother would call them—when somehow the blind-spots and worse among all too many psychiatrists are more than balanced by here a luminous word, and there an almost heroic deed. Yet, we must expect to live our lives uphill, and maybe, too, we ought write uphill; that is, we ought write in such a way that we take on the mysteries and tragedies and evils of this world, and only then acknowledge the joy that nevertheless (but only nevertheless) persists. All of which means that we owe one another whatever effort we can make: so that life will go on; so that we will be spared as much pain as possible; so that we will be saved from at least some of the nonsense that is everywhere; so that we will be granted those moments of courage and nerve, however brief—when for all the failures, for all the "problems" we see in ourselves and our neighbors, it is possible to say yes, and feel it enough to keep on trying.

Painful Creatures

Ann Beard

Ann Beard studied music in Kentucky, New York City, and India. She is presently Children's Project Director, Plymouth Settlement House, Louisville, Kentucky, and is a member of the editorial board of *Katallagete*.

There was no ingenuity that fear or a depraved imagination could devise which was not employed to break their spirit and satisfy the lusts and resentment of their owners and guardians—irons on the hands and feet, blocks of wood that the slaves had to drag behind them wherever they went, the tin-plate mask designed to prevent the slaves eating sugar-cane, the iron collar. Whipping was interrupted in order to pass a piece of hot wood on the buttocks of the victim; salt, pepper, citron, cinders, aloes and hot ashes were poured on the bleeding wounds. Mutilations were common, limbs, ears, and sometimes the private parts, to deprive them of the pleasures which they could indulge in without expense. Their masters poured burning wax on their arms and hands and shoulders, emptied the boiling cane sugar over their heads, burned them alive; buried them up to the neck and smeared their heads with sugar that the flies might devour them.

C.L.R. James, *The Black Jacobins*

Reflections are painful creatures. In America, there is a conscious conspiracy against all forms of creative thought for fear that one's mind might be freed, and thus become of no value whatsoever to capitalism, country, and Christianity (one and the same).

Nonetheless, reflection is necessary. It is necessary to share what has happened to us personally if for no other reason than that we might see that our experiences are not personal, but, rather, part of a larger blueprint.

I should have known better. (She said to walk eight blocks south. Building is on the right hand side). Anxious. Excited. First job. Right out of college. ("We'll be waiting for you," she said in her silk underwear voice.) Discovered myself in college. Talked, walked, thought blackness all the time! ("Yes, we are a negr...errr... Black agency.") Now to *use* it. With my people. Youth director. For my people. A chance to really do something.

I should have known better. Seven months later, no job. "What went wrong?" I asked as the big bird of technology flew west away from the scene of it all. Contradictions. The huge poster on the wall in the lobby read:

PURPOSE:

To respond to the barrier-breaking love of God in this day. To draw into responsible membership women and girls of diverse experiences and faiths, that their lives may be open to new understanding and deeper relationship and that together they may join in the struggle for peace and justice, freedom and dignity for all people.

After seven, long months, the purpose read:

1. To provide chummy staff luncheons at plush restaurants where all the ladies may talk about their diets.
2. To provide for even chummier board meetings where the "junior-leaguer" board president from "cross town" may show off her latest knit and Miss Ann accent, and where all the other "cross towners" and would-like-very-much-to-be-negro-cross-towners sip tea and are simply *thrilled!* over all there is to be thrilled over in America. ("See, Annie, the races here in Horseville get along so well together.")
3. To stage huge membership drives so that the feeling becomes "anybody who IS somebody" belongs to the XKYZ.
4. To entertain the almost-bourgeois with oriental dinners and provide ample opportunity for them to ask unknowing questions about China and Japan.
5. To provide the first-for-our-town Black director

with prestige, for a pet poodle and Cadillac are not
sufficient.
6. To maintain at whatever expense shiny floors and
polished silverware.
7. To provide another mechanism through which Black
people may be controlled.

Act II. Enter stage front left onto a state commission on
human rights. Huge poster on office wall reads:

PURPOSE:

*To insure the civil and human rights of all the great
people of this great commonwealth without regard to
race, color, creed, national origin, sex or age. Discrimination is defined as any refusal or denial to any person
to any goods and services because of race, color, creed,
national origin, sex or age. All individuals have the right
to be free of humiliation and free of indignities.*

After ten months, the poster read:
1. To provide employment for white executive director
at $16,000 so that he might live well in suburbia,
and so retreat when necessary.
2. To provide employment for all other whites who
mouth humanity and live like hippies. If possible,
allow both director and white staff members to
attend law school on company time.
3. To totally frustrate all Black employees, and to
make the environment so hostile and racist that they
are forced to leave in order to maintain dignity and
sanity.
4. To assure the Black community that everything possible is being done to abolish racism. To assure the
white community that racism will continue as usual.

5. To make proclamations, issue press releases and statistical reports and make once-a-year visits to the Black community to provide Black people with data and information which is guaranteed to promote a negative self-image. I.e., to provide another mechanism through which Black people are controlled.

All that changed was me. Despite all the empty staff meetings and "conferences to talk about me," I was all that changed. One of these institutions was private, the other public. One claimed to be Christian; the other an agency for the people. Yet I found no qualitative difference in the two. What this indicates to me is that we are still living on a great plantation. The existence of this plantation explains why all the efforts, energies, contributions of all those people with the very best of intentions are eventually used against them and the things they stand for. A "conspiracy" suggests that which is difficult to discern, uncover. What is happening in the United States of America is far from undercover. Some of us are confused (yes, indignant!) when we start to talk about all this simply being an extension of the plantation system. We are confused and indignant because we have been programmed to think that this is the freest country on the planet earth. Thus, everytime the tube is turned on, we see some jive-time freelance reporter doing a "special" report on China or Russia or Europe in which most of his rambling has something to do with the "people here in Russia or China" not having all the freedoms or supermarkets or beauty shops that we have. Everything which goes on on a plantation— be it food production, Saturday nite parties, floggings, "free time" for the slaves—everything is directed towards the growth of that plantation. This accounts for many so-called Black movements and movements "by the people" literally being turned around, and made into something totally different from their original form.

I can remember all too well the zeal and energy with which Black students in colleges and universities across this country set out to build Black studies departments. They were searching for tools to liberate, not jive-time joints to hang around in 'til all hours of the night. After all, the administration buildings had been taken over, and whites had grown accustomed to such tactics, the U. S. government moved all its resources onto college campuses—provided monies for books, lecturing Black professors, equipment, and stipulated guidelines, procedures and methods, and then made available thousands of dollars in scholarships—to KEEP THE NIGGERS IN THEIR PLACES.

And so the Black people and Black communities which had looked to these students and their organizations for direction and resources soon began to say among themselves, "Man, them brothers up there on that college hill ain't up to nothing. They just wanna party all the time." And the greatest power which slavery possesses, the power to make the slave end up hating and destroying himself and his kind, was set into motion. The seeds of division and distrust had taken root. This is the horror of horrors: that we should become like the enemy, that we are all at once field niggers and house niggers, that we are taking part in the oppression of our people. All of that brain power which is imprisoned on college campuses, taking advantage of fellowships and foundations, doing research on almost everything and his mama, is being used to further oppress the peoples of this earth.

For instance, I am told about a research project now going on in Washington, D. C. in which government and foundation monies are being used to study the effects of high rise, overcrowding, living on human beings. Rats are being used in this study because they respond in much the same manner as human beings to the various stimuli. This program was billed as a step toward solving the housing problems in urban areas. Black graduate students and others who were interested in "doing something" for their people poured in to work on the project.

Certain variants were controlled, such as food supply, fresh air, density population, drug supply, and "recreational" facilities. The theory was that if variants such as these could be controlled, then behavior itself could be controlled. For instance, when conditions were worst—filthy air, scarcity of food, plentiful supply of drugs, extreme overcrowdedness—the researchers found that the rats began to attack and destroy each other, even the baby rats clawed at each other's throats. They began to fight over what little food there was, and to crave drugs.

Contrary to what they were told, this and similar studies were used *not* to build housing which would guarantee against such acts. These studies were used to build housing that met certain specifications in order to guarantee that the occupants would end up destroying each other. Check it out. In every city across the country where housing is being built for Black and poor people, even the uneducated eye can see that in two or three years that housing will be slums. In other words, the United States of America is guilty of premeditated murder.

Black people in every condition find themselves making compromises. Black stars and entertainers find themselves on goodwill tours and singing under the armpits of Billy Graham and Richard Nixon at White House prayer breakfasts. Black athletes find themselves in half-time ceremonies with Miss White Peachpetal of 1909 hanging onto their arms. Giants such as John Coltrane and Charlie Parker find themselves torn between listening to the drums of their ancestors and making spiritual music, or recording music which white recording engineers liked and can sell. A Black teacher finds himself confronted with teaching the truth and endangering his own career or teaching "how-to-make-it-in-America-in-six-amazingly-difficult-steps" and endangering the very existence of all who sit at his feet. In each of the job situations that I have described, I found myself finally confronted with the alternative of doing something or doing nothing. Doing nothing is easier, but the price we pay could be the very survival of our spirits and souls.

There was a small privileged caste, the foreman of the gangs, coachmen, cooks, butlers, aids, nurses, female companions, and houseservants. These repaid their kind treatment and comparatively easy life with a strong attachment to their masters, and thus enabled Tory historians to represent slavery as a patriarchal relation between master and slave. Permeated with the vices of their masters and mistresses, these upper servants gave themselves airs and despised the slaves in the fields. Dressed in cast-off silks and brocades, they gave balls in which, like trained monkeys, they danced minuets and quadrilles, and bowed and curtseyed in the fashion of Versailles.

C.L.R. James, *The Black Jacobins*

The slavery under which we now live in America is mental slavery. The chains are so tightly drawn that we would not recognize truth if it were to walk up and slap us on the right shoulder. In fact, this is precisely what truth is doing now: staring us in our faces. And we cannot/will not recognize it.

Finally, that eternal question: "But what can I do now?" It stands to reason that if we are suffering because of mental slavery, then the task must begin with the mind, with awareness. This is an insane world in which we live. It is ridiculous to ask the insane to become sane; it is ridiculous to ask the oppressor to free the oppressed. The job of freeing the mind, of becoming aware, of removing the chains from our spirits, is a job each of us must consciously do for ourselves. We must study, reflect, study and reflect. We must come to grips with values which place life before all other things. We must strive for internal balance, so that we are not thrown off by marches and demonstrations, TV and magazines, Olympic games, Miss America, phony reports by presidential commissions, filthy air and water, big time vocations, federal programs and guidelines, faculty and staff meetings, Walter Cronkite, Miss Jones next door, American Cancer Society, Christian institutions, wife swapping, living bras, and weather reports. As the church people say but do not mean or understand: WE MUST WITNESS to life, to sanity, to total liberation.

> *But I am bound with you in your mean graves,*
> *O Black men, simple slaves or ruthless slaves.*
> Claude McKay

It Is a
Good Day To Die

Vine Deloria, Jr.

Vine Deloria, Jr., a Standing Rock Sioux, is the author of *Custer Died for Your Sins* and editor of *Of Utmost Good Faith*, a documentary case of the American Indian against the government of the United States. He is former Executive Director of the National Congress of American Indians, has been a member of the Board of Inquiry on Hunger and Malnutrition in the U. S. A., and of the National Office for the Rights of the Indigent. He has degrees in theology and law and has taught at Western Washington State College in Bellingham, Washington.

The editors of *Katallagete* have placed a very difficult topic before us, especially those of us who have suffered severe dislocations in our outlook in the last several years. Vocation in the old sense was a happy way of justifying working for a corporation while maintaining membership in the better Christian denominations and chastizing those who neither belonged to a denomination nor worked for a corporation. I first became aware of the concept of vocation when I asked our college chaplain at Iowa State if we could study Albert Schweitzer's *The Quest of the Historical Jesus.* He was horrified, as good college chaplains always are, told me not to question my faith, and advised me to find a Christian vocation instead of worrying about expanding my knowledge of Christian origins.

The word *vocation,* consequently, has always had a connotation of the closed mind in my reference system of emotionally-loaded words. Vocation has taken on the unfortunate value of being opposed to personal inquiry and I have always thought of the idea of vocation as something you do when your brain ossifies. A vocation, in the traditional sense, was an occupation based upon the consumption sometime in the distant past of a certain quantity of academic material. If one were very serious about the consistency of this content then one would naturally question the validity of the vocation also. I have not always been dreadfully happy about the world as I have known it and so have not been very eager to base a vocation on the content of knowledge about the world which is now available to us.

I consequently avoided the whole issue of vocation by working as a welder in a machine shop at night while attending a Christian seminary by day for four years. I wanted to discover if they who had preserved the faith to the saints once delivered had any thoughts on the world, which necessarily included vocations, or anything else for that matter.

The assumption that one must make, unfortunately, upon entering seminary is that due to a variety of circumstances, benign or malevolent, one has the inside track in comprehending divine mysteries. The tension, then, between keeping one's mouth shut in order to further explore the presence and knowledge of divinity, and launching a preaching career thereby solving all of the world's problems, increases as the seminary experience broadens. The posture of the seminary as repository of ancient and self-evident truths only increases one's sense of belonging to an elite which has been mysteriously ordained to promulgate the ground rules of the game of life, occasionally calling the fouls, but generally winking at minor transgressions confident that they are being recorded up above anyway.

One of the most heart-rending tensions of attempting to learn about the variety of religious experiences and doctrines is finding the proper guideposts in the world by which one can validate his behavior, in order to assure himself of the universal nature of the religious experience. Does doctrine precede and point to experience, or is it the abstraction and crystallization of experience? The difference is startling when one considers it. Doctrines based on experience are virtually useless unless people can discern from their contemporary situation patterns of behavior and answers of another age and place that appear at least compatible. Unfortunately doctrines and creeds involve little more than learned responses to classic situations where sin is not only apparent but gleefully participating. They may be proper and respectable slogans for affluent people to endorse but I have found them to be virtually useless for solving the brutal problems of everyday life. In retrospect, when one is pondering a problem which has been resolved, a conclusion that doctrinal elements might have been present is always a possibility.

Doctrines that precede experience, as ultimate revelation must certainly require, cannot exist without alternative interpretations available for the reflective person. To have followed a rigid doctrinal behavior and then learn of a not-so-doctrinal shortcut or alternative answer is the most destructive acid a doctrine can encounter. And the predictive nature of revealed theological concepts is totally crushing when the church does not act like its definition, and the pastor, priest or minister reveals himself as a fund-raising agent of the establishment and not a prophetic figure of the ages.

Thus seminary, in spite of its avowed goals and tangible struggle with good intentions, provided an incredible variety of food for thought but a glaring lack of solutions or patterns of conceivable action which might be useful in facing a world in which the factors affecting human life shift daily. The premise upon which religion and religious experience appeared to have rested prior to my seminary years—a final and unifying explanation of the meaning of life—was at once too general to be useful and too specific to be meaningful in the novel events of the 1960's and beyond.

Perhaps the best summary I can give of the intellectual content of seminary is that it appears to be more a hopeful bolstering of ancient dogmas and doctrines than a true exploration of man's spiritual problems and yearnings. Seminary projects, and one learns to analyze, problems in sets of questions and answers. Yet in life we dare to live in a condition in which both questions and answers continue to appear and never intersect or relate to each other. The solutions we find to pressing daily problems rarely come into the arena of creedal surety. The answers we find in the heat of battle and the quiet of meditation are answers to questions we did not think we asked.

After four years virtually devoid of revelation and sparse of even elementary information, I emerged into the real world confident that I had, if not the answers, at least the edge in my encounter with the world. The trauma was enlightening. People, it seemed, really didn't think about anything other than their jobs and their projected future which was in a constant state of migratory mortgaging. I passed rapidly into the world of national politics in the American Indian community. The novelty of political action and the solution to specific problems forced me to the conclusion that concepts used in analyses of problems could not be separated from one's knowledge of life itself.

It was only after I had experienced the same problems a number of times, but guised in different clothes each time, that I grew somewhat lazy and began to examine potential patterns of behavior rather than the peculiarities of the events themselves. The ability to predict with certain limits the breadth of the problem, the possible factors involved, and the conceivable leverage points at which problems could be revolved into soluble situations made it seem that at some point a final solution to certain consistent errors of mankind could be devised.

Having entered seminary thinking that religion was real and discovering upon graduation that it had little or nothing to do with life in the manner of which life presented itself, I rather naively entered law school determined to find a constant from which new vistas of humanity could be constructed. The whole tenor of American society has been to advocate a reliance upon the intangible and neutral operations of law to the exclusion of human frailties. Thus where religion could not provide any ultimate values for human life, law could at least provide a resting place and a temporary respite from conflict. Or so I thought.

Anglo-Saxon law and its bastard descendant American common and statutory law are consistent only so long as they remain unexamined. Upon any extensive inquiry into the philosophical or ethical basis for law as we know it, one encounters magic, mystery, and an incomprehensible jungle of conflicting statements about man and society. If theology is abstract with respect to this world and its problems, law is like pasting together pieces of eight different maps and then trying to build a threshing machine from the result.

The hope that law holds out to the uninitiated is that it gives answers to immediate problems and provides a sense of orientation in the situation man finds himself in, which answers and orientations if not satisfactory, are at least reliable for the foreseeable future. Law appears as a means of ordering our daily universe by clarifying the relationships we enjoy and suffer with others.

Graduation from law school returned the same message as had graduation from seminary. Law was even less related to life than theology. Law was so dependent upon a sense of integrity in the ultimate meaning that to speak of legal matters became, in the last analysis, an effort to discover theological presuppositions of men's action. But the possibility that the law can be manipulated, the dimensions of which had not been vaguely suspected until Richard Nixon and John Mitchell promulgated their concepts of constitutional rights, makes law a demonic force unless welded to a theological conception of man.

What can be said of theological education with respect to salvation can be said manifold in legal education with respect to the concept of property. Both appear to be the primary question and final answer of their respective systems. As absolute values they determine the way that we pose questions, that we analyze problems, and the manner in which we determine in our own minds which side we must take in the conflict. Having consumed this absolute during his first year in law school, the student is then forced to reconsider the implications of his knowledge by refuting his definitions for two years by learning the various fields of law which all refuse to relate to property and form a coherent whole.

Of the two types of education, legal education is by far the most crippling to one's mind. In the real world, rights emerge as a limitation on man's experience and not as guides to intelligent activity. The sudden and forced knowledge that *might* really does make *right* in the world as we experience it creates in many sensitive young lawyers a burning desire to advance the cause of justice. That justice is, in the last analysis, a temporary balancing of relative powers to create a more equal confrontation of unequal forces, is a bitter realization.

The incompleteness and fantasy of religion as we know it today drives one to believe in the efficacy of law as man's best hope for meaningful existence. (Witness the comparative numbers of people entering law schools and seminaries.) Law requires no supernatural stamp of approval for its existence, no esoteric revelation for those who would tread its bidden path. Yet law is hollow and without satisfaction when divorced from the moral and ethical sensitivities one must acknowledge exist. A legal victory devoid of moral or ethical satisfaction, although absolutely correct on legal grounds, would be the ultimate disaster. The relationship between law and religion, then, is a complementary one with each ultimately pointing at the other as the binding thesis of its existence.

In identifying this relationship, however, I absolutely and positively do not mean to relate it to the traditional Christian word game of the relationship between law and gospel. In the western world we have committed ourselves to an explanation of phenomena as basically evolutionary, that is to say, that phenomena grade themselves in time and project an increasingly better or more sophisticated pattern. From this evolution we necessarily place value judgments at certain points thus enabling ourselves to define the *progress* of the evolutionary process at any given chronological moment. In a substantial portion of traditional Christian efforts to relate law and gospel, law is considered as the evolutionary basis of preparation of gospel. Aside of the obvious twisting of the concept of law to include dietary and cultural requirements of the Hebraic Law, the relating of law to gospel implies that gospel is always in a position to act as judge on the operations and conclusions of law.

I would vigorously deny that the relationship between the law or laws of a society and its religion or the religious sentiments and experiences of a society consists of a judgmental position by either on the other. A totally consistent religious sensitivity sails by law and legal theory as if it did not exist. Law can be totally administered from any set of premises providing that those administering it maintain its purpose clearly in their minds. The integrity of one relates to the integrity of the other in that both are experiential fields including both individuals and social groups. An inconsistency experienced in any field of human affairs reflects as detrimentally on all other facets of the totality of the experience as does the apparent breakdown between law and religion.

In accepting the western evolutionary scheme of interpretation we have traditionally been forced to conclude that customs are a precursor of law in that they regulate behavior without being formally codified. Evolutionary interpretation would maintain that as society becomes more abstract and the need for information on customs is seen, laws become formal instruments promulgated abroad so that they cannot be manipulated to the benefit of those in power.

I would advocate an examination of the customs of a society as the basic requirement of understanding both law and gospel. At that point when customs have been adequately examined, one can lay customs aside and enter the twin fields of law and religion (or gospel in a Christian context) and identify them as components of a constantly shifting value scheme of both individuals and societies. Decision-making using one criterion precludes use of the same situation used in the same way by the other. One can be intimately aware of the implications involved in deliberately choosing to characterize a situation as having more similarity to one field than to the other. But to categorize one's choice as necessarily determined by the superiority of gospel or moral demands is to mesmerize oneself.

Perhaps the clearest examples of these situations come today in the protests against the war, the experiences we have suffered in the belated Civil Rights movement, and the question of amnesty. In characterizing one's behavior as a response to a higher moral requirement one should be damn sure that one's opponents understand and agree to the ground rules. The Milwaukee protesters burned the draft board files and claimed that it was a symbolic protest against the war. The District Attorney filed charges against them for breaking and entering. The symbolism was pleasing but did not communicate the moral issue the protesters thought they were raising.

A society appears to me to balance its sense of identity and integrity by altering the allegiances it pays to laws and customs at any particular period of its existence. In transferring its emotional identity toward law it requires further elaboration of its religious explanations in a theoretical or creedal sense. To place the concept of vocation in this mixture as a term descriptive of choice, deliberate or unconscious, would appear to be the greatest peril to mental health and psychological identity of both individuals and societies.

Preparing a statement on vocations, then, necessarily

involves determining at what point a person can find the interpretation of the world that provides him with a sense of personal identity and integrity. That is not to say that integrity is always a rigorous exercise of emotions or mentality or that a person can always act with consistency. One need only know that he is violating his own sense of identity and be able to evaluate his actions against his beliefs, abstract and tangible. Here I am not advocating an ethics of relative values. Right and wrong are generally a fairly clear choice, given the situation we confront. Occasionally deliberately choosing to violate one's own sense of being confirms in large measure that one is sane. The traditional picture of Jesus as a man who never acted against his own nature is rather bland and does not fit our experiences as we know them. As an exposition of the gospel it is senseless.

Preparing a conclusion, therefore, as to the meaning of vocation, is to allow the desperate balancing act of a sense of justice (however conceived), an experience, not an eternal surety, or identity, and a continual confrontation of the tough practical problems of the immediate situation emerge. The traumatic possibility that flying saucers exist, that mankind has experienced many diverse and tragic social movements that had apparent religious sanctifications but collapsed, and that once starting to redefine the world one can only find a temporary respite from the task of discovering oneself, may compose the phenomena we once abstracted as the basis for outlining a theory of vocations.

In recent years I have reluctantly come to the conclusion that nothing is really without a sense of purpose. In some obscure manner there appears to be a plan of overwhelming dimensions operating to bring us to certain plateaus of personal and social identity. I am not at all sure that this barely-detected plan is benevolent or that it carries any negative or positive values as we are accustomed to projecting. I am only convinced that on occasions it can be said to be beneficially revealed as constructive. At other times it appears that our own vision greatly surpassed what was actually possible or at least what was finally realized.

My present activity, for one could not say either occupation or vocation, (the tedious nature of routine is studiously avoided at all costs) is simply existing as a member of a partially-defined community. The community is an Indian tribal situation which fluctuates between memories of an exotic past and a precarious future defined in derogation of that past. I find so many similarities to other groups in the present Indian situation that I am tempted to say that I exist as a rural person partially consumed by future shock and badly crippled by too much education. Being a member of this community involves a certain tension between a willingness to share its happiness and grief and the personal demand to be its severest critic and most disloyal member, for I can even yet see the clouds of turmoil forming on the horizon.

American Indian people are presently faced with almost certain extinction of their land base and legal rights, and this is bad. But it is strangely enough, not evil. That Indian people might have not sufficient strength to survive this projected loss would necessarily require a judgment that my own community is not fit to survive. If the realization should come to that, I would somehow have to share our created evil. The problem is never to surrender to either possibility, success or failure, but to accept the fact that somehow peoples come and go and it is their experience of themselves in retrospect that is ultimately important.

In the Indian community there has always been the acknowledgement that living cannot be postponed. Particularly among the Sioux Indians, anything that has an identity calls men and societies to it. "It is a good day to die," Crazy Horse used to call as he rode out into battle. People accepted his challenge and followed him because he called into question their highest memories of themselves. If there is a sense, then, in which a person can have a vocation, it is to ride into one's community with a challenge to its presuppositions, presuppositions which one cherishes and from which one's identity is received.

If vocation is to exist in today's world it must certainly involve a heady willingness to struggle for both long and short term goals and at times simply for the joy of getting one's nose bloodied while blackening the other guy's eye. I would conclude that vocation has nothing to do with jobs, divine callings, political platforms, or wisdom and knowledge of the world. It is the solitary acknowledgement that the question of man's life and identity is to let the bastards know you've been there and that it is always a good day to die. We are therefore able to live.

A Letter
...and a Reply

Terrance Todd
Edgar Z. Friedenberg

Terrance Todd is Professor of Education at Mercer University, Macon, Georgia; Edgar Z. Friedenberg is Professor of Education, University of Dalhousie, Halifax, Nova

Scotia, and the author of many essays, reviews and books, including *The Coming of Age in America* and *The Vanishing Adolescent*.

Dear Edgar:

Early last month, when you and Judy and Bev visited us here at the Millhouse, we talked about a good many things, almost all of which bore at least a tangential connection to what I hope to make the heart of this letter. Maybe we can talk of this again when I come up to see you in Nova Scotia later in the Fall, but for now let me start out by trying to tell you a little more about the interrelationship between my home here in the country, my work at the university, my family, and me than I told you when you were down.

About three miles west of here Little Deer Creek crosses the old Taylor place and then joins with and becomes Deer Creek which continues on through the woods until it gathers strength by merging with and becoming Rum Creek which runs as you know almost under my house. We had a good rain last evening and so the sound of falling water that Judy said was like a steady surf comes to me fullvoiced as I sit at my table by the open window. It's the first of September in Georgia and the wind has with it the first edge of Fall. All of my family—Jean; my brother-in-law Frank; my sister, Connie; and my nephew, Timothy—are asleep now as it is very late and so I am alone with the sound of falling water, the smell of late Summer, and the task of shaping from words some semblance of myself.

I'm not sure I know how to do this. One thing I do know is that this wonderful old Millhouse and the land and stream accompanying it are beautiful to me in a way beyond my skill to tell. I know another thing. I know that they would almost surely not be registered in my name at the Monroe County courthouse had I not undergone the process (Do you recall the use of the word "process" to describe the hair treatment used by black folks to punish and manipulate their hair until it behaved in a way quite obviously contrary to its nature?) of higher education.

One thing I don't know or at least can't justify is how a person no older than I and possessing no inherited wealth could, leaving aside should, possibly own such a piece of property. Had I learned in college anything that, on its own, a reasonable man might consider valuable, perhaps I could begin to understand or even justify my ownership of house and land; but of course I learned nothing of the sort. What I did learn was that there *was* a direct connection between being in college and ever having the choice of owning such a place. Only later, after I left school and began my education, did I begin to see some of the implications of what I had learned. You were chief ophthalmologist.

And here I finally am with you, sitting upwind from the assend of the lectern, growing increasingly leery of my role as professor or, more precisely, of the role *of* professor. You remember, I'm sure, how Boaz explained himself to Unc in Vonnegut's *The Sirens of Titan* by saying that, "I found me a place where I can do good without doing any harm, and I can see I'm doing it, and them I'm doing good for know I'm doing it . . ." Barely credible as it may now seem, I actually did have a couple of years in which I believed that in college teaching I had found me such a place. So long ago.

I guess what brought it all home for the first time was an experience I had with a small class of undergraduate students at Auburn University a few years back. They were what would be called in some circles an "ideal" class—meaning, I suppose, that they were enthusiastic, bright, worked well together, and seemed genuinely to like my way of handling things. As an ironic validation of this, I was told subsequent to the end of the quarter that the class had drawn up and unanimously signed a statement addressed to the dean which said that they had learned more from the course than from any course they'd ever had, that they had also enjoyed themselves enormously, and that I was the best instructor under which it had ever been their privilege to study, etc., etc. The dean himself showed the statement to me under circumstances which, had I known them would have at that time been puzzling to me. The circumstances were that the very same dean who proudly shared with me the students' praise was simultaneously in the process (there's that word again) of assisting in the arrangement of events which would leave me with very little choice but to resign, establishing once again the fact that if you have a bit of conceptual dissonance that needs handling, get ahold of an administrator of any of our modern institutions and he can, I guarantee, take care of bidness. They sure took care of mine. Reminiscent of Nixon eulogizing the war dead. Or Crisswell sermonizing on reconciliation. Or Todd placing *Deschooling Society* on the reading list for his course (required for teacher certification) in Foundations of Education.

The point of all this is not, God knows, to trot out my liberal credentials, but to frame the background for a discussion of a little conceptual dissonance of my own. In the midst of my Boaz period when I was shown the statement the students had written, I found myself one day happily reviewing, in light of the statement, the events of the class when I remembered something I'd selectively forgotten. I remembered that one morning during the previous quarter after what had seemed to me to be an exceptionally successful class, I asked the students to decide what we should do the next day—go more deeply into what we'd been animatedly discussing or simply take a day off. Guess what they decided? I tried it again later in the quarter with the same result.

In my review of all this after the quarter, the unanimity and vigor of the vote for holiday began more and more to collide with the substance of the students' statement until finally even an old boy like me, kindly slow and all eat up with hubris to boot, began to put it together. The fact of the business is that a group of 15 young people, mostly seniors, who were supposed to be attending the university to gain wisdom, insight and reflectivity, when presented with a choice between attending a class which they unanimously agreed was the best they'd ever had and not attending the class, chose, every manjack there, not to attend. And you know what, Edgar? I was glad. And once I understood the one thing and admitted the other, I've been a changed man. So it goes.

To be truthful, I'll admit that I tried a few times to get back into my Boaz mood, but my heart, the *sine qua non* of a Boaz mood, just wasn't in it. Given that analysis, what does a man do? I'd already blown my big chance several years before by saying no to a filthy lucrative contract to enter professional wrestling. I turned it down because I felt called to become an educator. Professional wrestling might have made an honest man of me. But Edgar, when you're too old to break into the wrestling circuit and your eyes have widened to include a view of the functioning of other institutions, what do you do? Nothing on the outside that I could do looks much good. As you mentioned the other day in response to my remark that institutions these days just couldn't bear the load they were asked to bear, bearing the load may be less of a problem than the fact that no matter what load you're bearing and where you're going, there's already too much of it there when you arrive. A sort of universalized Newcastle.

As I told you last month, I'd as soon be Fred Wiseman as anyone, but I just don't have the courage to strike out on my own as he did. I am trying to do a little work on my courage these days, but it's mighty hard when you've paid as much of it out in tuition over the years as I have. Having the horizontally extended family that we have here at the Millhouse seems to me to be good for what ails all of us. It's especially good for me because I'm able to learn from my brother-in-law, Frank, who knows so much about so many physical things, but it helps us all because we learn to share the chores, we ride together to work, we try to become more considerate, and we talk these things out from time to time as we go along. We're trying to learn what our limits are for sharing, independence, and doing-without, so that we can begin to extend these limits little by little. We've seen so many folks come to grief by picking up more than they could pack off that we decided to do our best to find out what we could and couldn't do so that by doing what we could and sustaining one another we might be able to turn some couldn'ts into coulds. All very easy to say, of course, and quite probably self serving, but it seems to make at least a little sense and so here we are. Of course we all get our feelings hurt once in a while and either sull up or holler, depending on our style. I sull.

Being in the country is another aspect of my courage training. Having a little land to work, some woods to walk, a few animals to watch grow and the responsibility that it all entails all seems to me to be healthy. And it's good to have a place like this to share with your friends. All of these things may not be scientific objectives, but they do seem worthwhile.

I have a friend back in Texas, Edgar, who recently left college teaching and work on his dissertation because he said he began to feel he was paying a price he couldn't afford. He has a little tree trimming business now and has bought himself about 40 acres of bottom land on which he's planted several hundred pecan trees. He works hard at his job and he told me that it pleased him to be able to give a little more life to a tree and to be able to feel the pride of being fairly paid for a good day's work. He's doing a little poetry again. I've known him all my life and I've never seen him more at home with himself than he is now. I wish I was as much of a man.

But I'm not and may never be and so I'm back again to the same question, a question I've answered up to now by a yearly decision to remain within the institutional womb. I feel a bit like a farmhand who mused to himself one hot day while chopping a long row of cotton that, "You know, this sun's so hot, and this work's so hard, I believe I'm called to preach." So I remain in the institution, scuffling to make do. Whether this decision to remain results from a legitimate social philosophy, rationally arrived at after having carefully weighed the alternatives or from Marcuse's one dimensionality, what with the Millhouse and all, I'm not sure.

But the closer I look, the flatter I appear. I've been
getting by for the most part simply by trying to make
my work and the work of those with whom I share my
life space a little better. I've drastically lowered my
expectations. Of just about everything.

In that regard, I do, however, still believe that the
words "better" and "worse" have some contextual importance in an educational institution. One of the few
things happening now on our campus that seems positive is that there appears to be more discussion among
both faculty and students about a matter that should
be the driving wheel of any university—the nature of
education. I am now asked, by more students than used
to ask, my views on whether or not I regard as mutually
exclusive the term, "college education." In response, I
can say, do say and hope to be able to continue saying
that although college does lie on a dark prairie, there
are fires to be found at which warmth and sustenance
can be had for the asking. And that these fires may or
may not but probably won't have much or anything to
do with classroom work or outside assignments. And
that these fires are not so numerous that chance should
be trusted to turn them up. And that turning them up
may require sacrifice. And that to receive maximum
warmth and sustenance from those you find will almost
surely necessitate a certain disregard for the regular
academic program. And that this disregard has a price.
And that this price should be paid. And that the average
institution, such as a college, one might chance to meet
in this technolotrous society is without question a dangerous mother and should be seen for what it is and
resisted, as its aims are almost always in direct opposition to the enhancement and survival of any and all

opportunities to make true and human use of our human minds and bodies. And, finally, that they (the students) may (1) take what I say and use all or any part of it they need or want, (2) accept it *cum grano salis,* or (3) reject it completely.

A majority of the students thrown by fate and the computer into contact with me opt for either #2 or #3 above for a variety of reasons not the least of which is that, as any physiologist will tell you, twelve or fourteen years of confinement and inactivity tends to cause stiffness and frailty instead of flexibility and strength. But you do what you can. You arrange a variety of outside experiences in the schools for your students so that they can see more objectively the system through which they have come and how that system has both helped to make them what they are and hindered them from becoming what they might have been. You remember how you were yourself that first year in college and how much you wish someone had said to you then what you now try to say as clearly as you know how to these young folks with whom your life intersects and you say these things even though you suspect you would probably have heard no more willingly than they. But you do what you can out of a combination of concern for all of your students, hope for what some of them (and you can't always tell which ones) may become, and resentment for the years you might have put to better use.

In the Fall of the year 1972 Mercer looks, because of this discussion, just a little bit better to me than she did a year ago. For whatever reason, that's not an easy statement to make about an institution these days. Now that's not to say that I think this discussion will result in anything serious being *done* at this institution. You can, after all, eat only so much of your own foot. But it is better than it was and I believe I can live with that. At least for a little while longer.

Edgar, I've read and listened to you long enough to know that you don't sit all that easy in your endowed chair up at Dalhousie, and as I deal as best I can with the dilemmas of our profession, I often wonder how you've handled them over the years and how you handle them now. When you told me sadly that the freedom and self-determined grading procedures you gave the students your first year at Dal had attracted such a high percentage of second year ripoffs that you had decided to give some quizzes and other required work this year, my suspicion that insight into a problem doesn't necessarily include the problem's solution was confirmed. But then I never loved you because of your solutions.

I think I'll go downstairs now and fry some sausage and decide how to spend the rest of the day. I hope this letter finds you and your fine young folks well, and that my remarks provide at least a point of departure for your own analysis of how you're bearing up after 20 some odd years as a member of the world's second oldest profession.

Yours,
Terry

Dear Terry:

If I understand the problem, one reason that it is hard to solve is that it isn't a real problem; or rather, the conditions envisaged as possible solutions are unreal. The idea that most people could earn their living doing work they deemed useful and rewarding for roughly the same reasons that their society in fact rewarded them for it is, I suspect, valid only in (1) a "folk society" in which each man knows and practices the skills that every man does, which remain the same from year to year though they change from season to season, and whose value and relevance are seen to be self-evident; (2) vocations and professions in more diversified, complex societies which serve a relatively uniform social class and clientele whose values the practitioner shares or adopts. Democratic societies, however, have special problems with this sort of thing: for one thing, their egalitarian ideology keeps their members from identifying easily with the interests of a wealthy patron—corporate or individual—as he sets about exploiting poorer or less powerful people; for another, the intensely competitive character and relatively unstable status arrangements of modern open societies make it essential to self-esteem that people be well and conspicuously recognized and rewarded for the work they do, if they are to retain their identity.

The Americans who probably experience most congruence between what they do in their work and what they think they're spozed to do are lawyers like Clark Clifford who know quite well who they are working for and how good they are at their jobs, and who have understood from the beginning that the law is a set of adversary proceedings, so that it was to be expected that their client's adversary would be the worse for their ministrations, if they were any good. Designers for Neiman-Marcus probably find their work groovy, too; and Clint Murchison seems to be free of guilt that the new Dallas stadium puts football games beyond the reach of nearly all spectators except the rich subscribers who hold the bonds for its construction. But most of us are more ambivalent than that; we want to feel that our services are generally useful, and not the prerogative of a privileged class. There are several things that can be done about this; but they all seem to raise as many problems as they solve. The commonest, in commerce and the media, though not infrequently in the arts and professions as well, is to seek a mass clientele, directly and openly. That is what you would have done had you gone into professional wrestling. And don't knock it. I have a lot of respect for old Frank Yerby—though I'd probably have less if I read one of his books. But he turns out a quality-controlled product, gives consistent value for money, and knows his own name instead of calling himself Quadaffi 57 X or something. So he isn't a great author like Eric Segal; everybody can't be Jewish.

To a considerable, and rapidly increasing, degree this is also what colleges and universities are doing. The rhetoric refers, with some sincerity no doubt, to extending the opportunity to attend college to elements of the population formerly denied that opportunity and the privileges thereunto appertaining. Be that as it may, colleges, particularly urban colleges, are clearly under considerable pressure to maintain their enrollments and attract new political constituencies and sources of support by admitting students previously considered poor academic material, and usually from lower status backgrounds than their students used to have. The result is, however, increased incongruity between the professor's expectations and the satisfactions he actually gets out of the job. It isn't that the new students are necessarily less able, less interesting, or less moving in their needs; they may be superior in all these respects. But the whole process is cruder, more rushed, more instrumental; they are likely to be even less interested in the material than their predecessors and more interested in what they can use it for. One place I insisted Bev and Judy and I stop over on our way back from the Millhouse was Charlottesville, to visit the University of Virginia campus and Monticello. I was determined that they were to see these if they saw nothing else in the East. It shows what, for a time, it looked as if America might have become. That campus has always affected me most peculiarly. I know it was never a great university; but I also know that when I decided to become a university professor my unconscious had in it an image of a place just like that—though I never saw U. of Va. till I was nearly thirty—and was haunted by the memory of the insouciant young men who must have attended it. In retrospect, I can see it was stingy of me to try to skimp through this century with an old, used unconscious. Nevertheless, no community college, I'm sure, is ever going to make it with me the same way.

But there are worse things than catering to a mass clientele, even though a mass clientele is, by definition, already largely alienated and conditioned to raven after its proper bane. And what is, I think, worst of all is to have a purely captive clientele, which is to say not really a clientele at all; just a set of victims who have been defined by society as your beneficiaries but who know damned well they are expected to exist in order to serve you, not the other way around. This is now very common—perhaps the commonest way for the middle class to earn a living. And it really precludes almost any possibility of honest job satisfaction. And egalitarian guilt, curiously enough, has greatly accelerated this unfortunate process.

In American—or Canadian—democracy—whatever the government has left over after providing for the common defense is spozed to be used to promote the general welfare. Not very much is, of course; but what there is of it is essential to giving the government what little aura of legitimacy it has, so there are surely a lot of hassles over it. Considering the influence of the military-industrial complex, I would maintain that today the *only* difference between the public and private sectors of the economy is that the public sector is laden with guilt over its putative equal obligation to rich and poor alike, while the private sector is relatively guilt-free, and therefore probably relatively pleasanter and more forthright to work in. The Dow people never really believed they shouldn't make napalm—business is business—though they were finally talked out of it as bad PR. But schoolteachers really do think they are supposed to be of some use to the kids in their "opportunity" classes—though they also know they would be fired if they did their job so well that these kids became the winners and their academic, middle-class pupils the losers.

The trouble with institutions set up and pledged to serve people of all walks of life and degrees of social status equally is that the poor or underprivileged or whatever they're called this season really do lack political clout and often political smarts as well—whatever else they may be equal to what we may roughly call "white folks" at, they aren't equal in power—by definition. The people who service them are therefore always working for somebody else, really. They know quite well that their job security and advancement depend on their colleagues and their superiors, not their clients. This, of course, is what the "community control" issue is really about. But how can there be community control without community licensing and funding? The man who pays the piper gets, at least, to negotiate with ASCAP; the audience gets the choice of applauding or not applauding.

Consequently, each service cadre, by "professionalization," licensing, and so on, seeks to maximize its power to define the particular problems it ascribes to its clients. In return, it log-rolls by recognizing the corresponding rights of other cadres. The client, however, remains a passive consumer or victim if he is poor, or young, or adjudicated. But the younger, poorer, and more adjudicated he is the more egalitarian brownie points the profession gets by attending to his needs, where a bourgeois client would have the clout and the insight to try to insist on defining his own, which makes him more of a threat as well. Serving the rich is not only un-cool and undemocratic, it's also more dangerous: they're likely to know what they think they want, and all about malpractice suits.

Social democratic societies have, therefore, by now come to enroll their professionals in organizations whose real clients are, increasingly, one another. The teacher's referrals for counseling make it possible for the guidance-counselor to earn a living; the intolerably disturbed child is the one who insists he has no problems, needs no service, and doesn't mind being ignorant in school. Insurance companies cheerfully bear the burdens of enough litigation to support the nation's trial lawyers, and pass the cost on to the consumer in increased premiums. Medical specialists segment their patient into a bit of pathology for all. Students take my course for credits toward a credential that will license them to teach Nova Scotia children—though what I teach them is, in effect, that their work will almost surely do the children more harm than good. None of us sits down with a real client any longer, to begin by asking him: "What seems to be the problem? What is it that you feel you need?" The people who do this are people who cater honestly, though often superficially and nearly always within the limits of a mass economy with all its corruptions, to real clients who have real money, not just civil rights or vouchers: travel agents, restaurant managers, liquor salesmen. Colonel Sanders, by all accounts, is a happy man. He should be.

Why does the public put up with all this service whose function is primarily to make work for those who provide and administer it? Partly, as I have indicated, because egalitarian ideology makes a virtue of shoving most of it off on people who are too poor, too young, too black, or somehow too disfranchised to defend themselves. But also, I am sure, because most North Americans have been taught, in any case, to identify primarily with their job role. People don't think of themselves as pupils, defendants, patients—all these are thought of as temporary and recognized as vulnerable roles that don't bear too much consideration. They think of themselves rather as potential teachers, lawyers, doctors—our earliest indoctrination in school sees to this— and learn not to be a troublemaker and queer the salesman's pitch lest, touching it, they be defiled. Your account of your experiences with your students, Terry, seems to me to have little to do with your success or failure as a teacher, except that they clearly recognize you as good enough to make them willing to play their

supporting roles so you can play—in this production—
your stellar one. If, however, you raise the possibility
of "No performance today"—that's groovy, too! No
sweat.

As to how I personally manage? I don't have an
endowed chair. Just tenure, which is a kind of chair:
c'est un commode, mais c'est commode. (I live in a
bilingual country, and am permitted to do my business
in either official language.) And, to paraphrase Flan-
ders and Swann a bit, I do feel irrelevant. But I'm not
irrelevant, I'm an hippopotamus. That is, my students
do, I think, learn something of prurient interest but
redeeming social value by interacting with me. There
are not many of my kind in Nova Scotia—a handsome
place, physically, but resounding with the joyous abandon of more than half a million moderately unsuccess-
ful Scotsmen, who are seldom sufficiently open to
require the products of the enormous Scott Paper mills
that pollute the waters of Pictou Bay.

I don't know what I'm doing here; but sometimes I
think I know what I am being here. And, as Count
Dracula observed, home is where the heart is.

Yours,
Edgar.

A True Cowboy Story
and Why It Might Be a Lie

Steve Nickeson

Steve Nickeson is editor of *Race Relations Reporter,* Nashville, Tennessee.

The finest horse I ever rode was born when I was eleven and filling my mind with Greek legends. I named him Pegasus. But by the time he was five and ready to ride, I had tired of mythology, so I just called him Ole Horse. No one had ever tried to turn him into a four-legged human being, a task any horse will fail at; he thought like he was born to think. That didn't make him the most trustworthy animal, or the most pleasant ride. It just made him a hell of a horse.

The first time I ever rode him was to go after a three-year-old cow who had been a stray for about a year and had finally turned up running with a half-wild open range herd about three miles from our ranch on the Wind River Indian Reservation in Wyoming. Ole Horse and I came across her and a dozen others laying in the willow shade. They were a ringy bunch and we cued their stampede. But Old Horse knew what he was doing. He dispersed them and boiled all the action down to the three of us; that cow, Ole Horse and me, all careening along like we were possessed, in the opposite direction from home. Cow had a long lead, but Ole Horse was stretching out behind her like a hound. I was just along for the ride and to cuss the cow, cheer on the horse and hope to God he didn't fall.

Within a half-mile, Cow began to tire, lose coordination in her rear end and bawl with a fanatic rage for getting rid of me and Ole Horse. That was when she spun and came at us with her final solution. She was looking to kill Old Horse. I pulled him hard to the left and her meat fork horns only grazed his flank and hooked through his tail. Then she ran only far enough to gain momentum and took us on like before. Again I reined to the left, but I was forgotten. Old Horse had his own plan. He cut to the other side of her line of charge and when she shot past under his neck, he bunched up and shouldered into her ribs on a dead run. Her hind quarters whipped about like a turnstile, she went down, rolled over once and signed her truce.

We let her rest and by and by she got up voluntarily, turned and loped back to the ranch. Everything was to plan now and it was an easy peace just posting along at an unhurried distance behind. Not far from the ranch one of the young range cows decided to join us. She thought it was some kind of happy parade and she bucked and raced along beside our cow, thrilled to be relieved of the boredom of her day. I let the second cow come along rather than upset the intentions of ours, or take her mind off her direct route home. I would put both in the pasture and after another wild chase run the newcomer back out to the open range.

But it didn't work out that way. When we crested the last hill above the gate I had left open for our return, my serenity left and the profanity took its place. Just inches inside the gate was a black Volkswagen, bogged to the axels in an irrigation ditch. It was there because the vicar from the nearby Episcopalian mission and orphanage was a man who was careful to cover all his bets. On a Sunday morning he would beseech God for world peace, but just in case that was out of God's hands, in the afternoon he would go up and work on a fall-out shelter he was building into the side of an arid hill across the pasture we were bound for. This particular morning he had taken a newly arrived social worker up for an inspection of the digs. They hadn't counted on the full irrigation ditch and were so intent on getting out that they never saw my little procession or picked up my shouts. Finally they heard the hooves on the road and looked up to see these two wild-eyed cows racing close down upon them. Their immediate reaction was to start dashing aimlessly here and there, waving their arms and murdering my hopes of getting those two cows through the gate. But I had underestimated our cow's determination. She slid through by pivoting around the gate post like it was a part of her and was home. The newcomer wasn't quite so well motivated. Right inside the gate she braked hard, reeled back through it and fled. It couldn't have worked out better.

The vicar and the social worker scrambled to close the gate and were shaken and apologetic when I rode up. They thought neither cow was to go through. I assured them that everything was fine, but in their excitement they never quite understood my explanation. I suppose they thought I was being sarcastic or inordinately polite when I thanked them for their help.

That whole story is true and I have used it innumerable times in the dozen years since it happened. It really didn't have any moral to it, no lesson. It only worked to create an aura of glamor and maybe a little danger and to evoke a small laugh at the expense of two dudes. I don't tell it much anymore because I came to realize that it had no more accuracy than Ole Horse had wings. It was just another case of where facts, lifted out of years of context, produce more lies than a picture of the truth. I found the story didn't serve me or anyone else. It only fueled a hacked and self-defecting myth about a vocation and a way of life.

There is something about a myth that causes its makers and subscribers to go blind to the real people whom the myth is all about. The myth-maker is convinced that he is doing the subject a favor with his work. After he makes the pictures, the models are dismissed, forgotten. Supposedly, the tribute that will come the models' way will be payment enough for the sittings.

And so the models comply and forget that a legend is nothing more than gossip promoted to the ranks of institution. Part of the models' privacy will be translated into a rumor, and the rest, the veracity and integrity, will be swept aside and lost.

Myth making is an ancient skill designed to give people a goal or a hero or a day dream by making them think they are well-educated on a subject they really know nothing about. The New Left once gave itself purpose by creating a picture of a working man who never was. Country music gets money from non-traveling dreamers for singing about the journeys of a truck driver who never was. And an entire society once underwrote the conquest of half a continent by fabricating profiles of a Western rancher who never was. Myth making is a necessary game that would be almost entirely harmless except no one can live up to someone else's advertisements of them. Eventually the myth models will be shunted to one side in the believer's doctrinaire search for the genuine article. Those models who fall short of their role will be berated and those who come closer will be patronized.

People who keep track of such things tell us that the agrarian myth has been with us since that poet memorialized what he thought was the honesty, dignity and righteous simplicity in the man with the hoe in his hand. Most Western ranchers are still carrying around more than their fair load of that myth made heavier yet with the romance of the frontier. That legend has made use of any number of disguises in its pretense to be the truth and it will probably continue that way, healthy, long after the ranchers have disappeared. Especially now that they are an endangered species.

When a person grows up among the models for the

rancher myth, and has had experience along those lines himself, the myth's perimeters are beyond vision and its strength unknown. I never saw how big it was until I looked at it from two years away and four broad states to the east. Never having seen the extent of the myth, I had no immunity against it. So from the first it began to work its debilitating effects on my judgement. Although I was now a journalist who had never possessed a strong desire to be a rancher, I was flattered to have my background and my youth associated with the myth. And I was guiled by the apparent dignity which I had just discovered in that vocation. I had to go back and relearn a few things to realize the extent to which I had been conned.

But I wasn't alone, or the hardest hit. I was to see what it would do to a close friend who had grown up in the West, but never had any of the rural experience that from time to time would save me from the myth's more obvious lies. Jim had been cooped up too long in a Chicago graduate school, and that's where the myth seduced him. He ended up taking it, like a mistress, back to the land and to a job on a ranch in the southeastern mountains of Wyoming. In June of last year, he and his wife and the myth moved into a trailer house on that ranch and my wife and I dropped by not too much later to see them.

He couldn't have found a better ranch and the owner, Hank, was perfect. Zane Grey has written up his face, or faces like his at least once per novel. Hank was approaching 70. He was stooped from the hips and when he walked his elbows bowed out from his ribs and the palms of his hands always hung towards the rear. You can stand outside the Ag College of any Western state university and see an imitation of that walk performed precisely by almost any student there. The difference is that those students, if need be, can straighten up all their bones and muscles. Hank can't any more. I found that Hank had once known my father and his family some 50 years before and so we shared some mutual stories about speak-easy fights and rodeos and one particular good looking woman. He was a comfortable man to be with.

Hank had hired Jim with haying season in mind, but he had arrived at the ranch a week before that hard work season was to begin and so Jim got a taste of the more myth supporting work. He and Hank's foreman had been tearing around on the sage brush hills after cattle, branding calves. But it was all carrot and stick and it pulled Jim into the drudgery of making hay. But he didn't see it that way. To him it was going to be a splendid and ennobling time of experience and education that only contact with the land can bring.

His enthusiasm was indomitable. It survived even his association with the other temporary hay hands. There were four or five and only one was local and worked for Hank at other times. He was a sullen, aging, silent, misanthropic Scandinavian who no self-respecting myth would touch. The rest were winos who had been shipped up by bus from a skid row employment agency in Denver. The idea that there might be a tomorrow was about the most exotic abstraction their ruined minds could handle, no romance in their quarters either. It was obvious that dependability was not the highest requirement for employment at Hank's. While some of the winos would endure the entire bus ride up from Colorado, others would disappear along the way and Hank would have to phone down for more. But they had one reliable quality, the winos, they were in almost assembly line supply. If one disappeared or fell off the wagon, his replacement, like a tractor part, was no more than a few hours away. Hank didn't hire them because he felt sorry for them, or because he thought the work might be therapeutic. He hired them to be the cheapest pieces of machinery on the ranch. They didn't require much upkeep, a few meals and a cot, the wages were negligible. I don't think it ever occurred to Hank to like any of the winos. When he drew them into some foggy conversation it was out of bored curiosity or the need for some slight amusement. It was like the king playing straight man to the jester. If any of the winos were still sharp enough to pick up his motive they would forgive it for the small attention it would earn them and then too it might be one of the few chances they had to talk. For some reason there was a lot of hostility in the ranks and practically no communication. Every now and then, the myth will promote a story of a robust and rollicking hay or harvest crew, but Hank's outfit couldn't touch it. There was just too much of that animosity and too many cases of the shakes.

But that was no bother to Jim. He was in love with the beauty of the ranch and Hank looked like a hero. In his conversation, Jim could see himself content to live for years on a ranch like that and spent a good amount of time plotting the finances of his dream. I hinted that he should not invest too much, too soon. Haying is the kind of labor which can sweat the aspirations out of anybody. But I didn't press too hard, I was still under the influence myself and I could see that Jim had found a home. But I suspected that Jim thought I was being a little insensitive toward the vocation and according to the myth, the extension of that would be that I was never fully rural. In a couple of days we went home too, and I began putting up the hay on my father's ranch.

It is a smaller ranch and one young man can handle the hay by himself with a couple of day's assistance from a neighbor. I found that my warning to Jim stood good for me. It did not take more than an hour to re-develop my perennial hate for the haunches-pounding bounce of a worn tractor seat or the smell of the exhaust during a long run into the wind. I soon reexperienced the hours of circular repetition and the search for the right clatter or squeak in the machinery to play rhythm to the songs that meandered incessantly through my mind. When the songs wore out I remembered how to talk out loud to myself and then to the tractor, the hay, the sage hens and then to nothing in particular. I was in for some more neck snapping, bone shocking rage when the tractor would hammer across a hidden prairie dog hole. Occasionally a breakdown would relieve the monotony and avenge me against the machinery, but it would also bring with it the slow frustration of having to operate with imprecise haywire repairs until the replacement part, like a wino, would arrive from town. And it was taking longer to walk away the stiffness of the day than it ever had before.

But I also became reacquainted with the kind of simplicity and solitude that can be found just this side of boredom and that produced a softness that made me glad I was there. It was during the easy times of those days that I evaluated the different tasks on a ranch, not on their specific purpose or overall function, but on what the job gave a person and what that person had to pay. I remembered that handling livestock can be a pleasantly dirty and always varied exercise. There is a tactile excitement in wrestling a stout colt into his first halter or treating cattle for injuries and sickness. This excitement always carries with it rope burns, mashed toes and fingers and the threat of broken bones that always cloud man's dealings with intermittently tame animals. Putting up a fence is a tedious and time consuming job, but it provides the satisfaction of having constructed a well-built, functioning item. Empathy and imagination become crippling afflictions when it comes to castrating bull calves, but that can be forgotten with loud cynicism or the concentration over sharp knives and the techniques that prevent the animal from bleeding to death. There is nothing that can match the numbing, bloody urgency of jerking a too large calf out of its too small mother, but if the calf lives it can replace the presence of filth, cold and exertion with gladness and a little awe. I had left that ranch and returned enough times to know that repetition can erode the quality of enjoyment that is produced when the jobs are still novel. And so after years of it, each job is blended and blurred into a single vocation whose major satisfactions come from making a living and doing the whole thing well. Gradually the highs and lows are leveled out with a seasonal constancy. Snow makes misery in the winter and irrigation water in the spring when you brand the calves of the cows who were branded two or three or more years before. Next the hay is made and it is fed in the snow and so it goes around again.

There were a few days in mid-summer when we were ahead enough in our work to take a few days and drive down towards Colorado. That provided another chance to drop by Hank's ranch again. The first thing noticeable was that the beauty of the mistress myth was beginning to fade here and there. Jim explained that he had been operating a hay rake for the first day and a half of the season, but as soon as the first bales were made, Hank had transferred him to stacking them. He got the idea that as soon as a few more winos were recruited he would go back to a better spot to continue his ranching education. But the reinforcements were never mustered. Hank probably had good reason for this change. Jim was the youngest and healthiest member of the hay crew and it seemed logical that he would be doing the hardest work, but Jim was beginning to get the idea he might have been bought. Then too, he wasn't quite sure when he would be paid. He said he had recently started indulging his compulsion to stand atop the stack between bale deliveries and shout obscenities into the air.

What was left of Jim's dream had taken a slightly different perspective. He was now thinking that there were better possibilities in becoming a gentleman rancher. And he was wondering why Hank didn't operate with more efficiency, why he didn't have more respect for the winos and why he didn't regard the other hands more as human beings and less as employees.

About the first of September Jim and his wife repaid that visit. Jim was no longer returning to the land and he was now back on earth. He complained that on the evening he had stacked the last bale, Hank had come around with a check and a polite request that the trailer be vacated as soon as possible. No friendships had been made, no lasting contact established. It had all been a business transaction. Hank had paid attention to his end of it and Jim had been expected to do the same. When my father heard Jim's lament, he asked if he had been cheated. Jim said no, he hadn't. Then he was told he had no cause to complain. It was about a three sentence lesson that Hank, like any other rancher, didn't have the time or the money or inclination to bother with the preservation of a slightly inaccurate dream.

Jim had found that Hank was not a reincarnate myth. He was just another person, hiring, firing, building and destroying, buying and selling and trying to make a profit. Jim's contact with Hank had shown him that the old man's routine association with the land had not inseminated in him any seeds of superior wisdom nor largess. It had not endowed him with any honesty beyond that of the rest of the population. It had not alleviated him of any of the usual bigotries, irrationalities or pettiness that could just as easily characterize a banker or a plumber or an insurance adjuster. Jim had found that people like Hank don't live on the land and touch it daily for serenity, simplicity, intellectual stimulation or the cleansing of their souls. They do it because they are in the business. Their love of the land has little to do with the spiritual, it's more the love of pride and ownership.

And so men like Hank can become a disillusionment to the believer who finally sees that the rancher's standing as a man is based on his ability to perform his duties and make good on his word. But the death of the belief is not complete until the outsider sees that there is a standard proportion of ranchers who hate their vocation and neglect it, who steal from their neighbors, twist their children, beat their livestock and abuse their wives.

The myth and its eventual disappointments have no partiality to age. If you stay around that Western state university you will find that the ranchers' sons in that Ag College, the ones who are known as Cowboys, are a collective target of scorn from the liberal arts contingent. Of course it works the other way around too. The Cowboys, as seen by the more sophisticated students, are semi-literate, belligerent boors who have been left too long in a marinade of unenlightened conservatism and the pretensions of a Marlboro ad. They have betrayed the spiritual ethic of the land and have sold out to a mundane order of scientism, profit and technology. Those are sins, especially these days, and especially if one is a liberal arts student with a dream to return to the land and become part of that growing movement.

Those people, mostly young, mostly urban, who are returning to the land are motivated by ecological concerns and the means of surviving in their escape from metropolitan insanities, both of which are shaded here and there with a Deistic revival. God knows they have every cause to escape and survival is reasonable enough. No one has ever been hurt by a crash course in Emersonian self-reliance. However, the mythology and the religious aspects of their return have hidden from them the reality that land ownership and use and property rights are not naturally ordained to any man, but are created by whatever strengths a society prescribes for its own benefit and inherited by those people with the economic and political resources to protect them. Thus the back-to-the-landers are apart from those nonbelievers who still have to contend with each other, a market system they have no control over, and the perpetual competition that land, uninhabited by myth, always brings.

To a society that counts its wealth in monetary units,

land has always been more valuable than the people who happen to be owning it or working it at the time. But to many, that is a crass and embarrassing fact. Perhaps that is why the myth was made. Maybe it was needed to fabricate a little additional worth for those ranchers and farmers. Not for their own sake, but to make the other people a little more at ease, blind them to the models' expendability. Just as the myth can help create, it can be called upon, in a slightly different form, to let the survivors, the believers, down easy when the models' time has come. That's what's happening now. In books and in movies cowboys and old ranchers are losers these days, they can't conquer a thing. You can see that by dropping out to the drive-in to watch *Monte Walsh* or one of that *genre* or tuning into the fourth TV replay of *Lonely Are the Brave*. Those stories can supply the excuse for a few minutes of genuine sadness and they might even bring out that classic old worthless protest that "things will never be the same."

Things haven't been the same for years now. During the 1960's a million ranchers and farmers had to give up their land and move to town, just like the million who did the same during the decade before. That leaves 2.8 million and that number will be cut by better than half during the next eight years. Some people say that there will only be 500,000 ranchers or farmers left to own property by 1985. Any resemblance between them and the ones who remain now will be purely a product of tradition and imagination. The similarities will be a vestige of the myth. It will have little to do with the commonplace fact that agriculture has never been anything more than a task in which ordinary people supplied all the other ordinary people with food and fiber.

Now that reality is being dissolved away at both ends by two dissimilar factions who have borrowed only enough from agriculture to flavor their own original activities—activities that gave them an ace in the hole, the security to be the next to put their claim on the land. The men who devote their lives to industry, marketing and management have stepped into food production and have called it agri-business. On their end of it ranching and farming are not vocations, but commerce is. On the other end are the back-to-the-landers who have leap-frogged the subdivisions to indulge, in their own ways, the affluent and urban dream of Rural Living. They are convinced that vocation is secondary to the style of life. So ranching and farming is not a vocation there either, it is more like any hobby that consists of the by-hand growth or manufacture of consumables. Perhaps their end could be called agri-crafts. But whatever the terms, the "culture" suffix of the word is being left behind.

Actually, the society is not being reduced any by leaving the "culture" behind. There are the other two waiting to take its place; the "business" and the "crafts." Someday they will be respected and common vocations, each accredited with its own status and function and myth. The two will fall into the vocational fashion parade that has always come and changed and gone and always will as long as members of the human race occupy their time with habits that are of benefit to more than just themselves. If such an activity is a "calling" and not merely an occupation, then it will be of just that much more *benefit*. That's a lot to expect, though. It is a rare man or woman who is called by anything more than a country or a subculture, or their own stomachs, fears or vanity. Only when a habit is a calling will it give its practitioner much more than a fairly cheap and transitory meaning. If meaning is important, then most of us will have to look elsewhere.

At the end of one of the graceful, early days in September of last year, I was standing beside an almost completed span of new corral, finishing up some chores before we were to leave the ranch again for the East. On an overturned bucket a transistor radio was playing Glen Campbell's song about the last time he saw some woman's face and I was using that as cadence while I secured the biggest of the corral rails with some foot-long spikes and a 12 pound sledge. Down the slope 100 yards were two men—my father and a fellow who had worked with us for gratis or for pay, on and off, for the last 20 years. They were putting the last touches on a summer's irrigation, talking it over. The two of them had started that new corral, but had left the spikes and the sledge to me, and for good reason. Together they were crowding 140 years of life. They combined enough arthritis to paralyze a single man, or enough emphysema to kill him. There was a handful of various unbending fingers and a fraction over two good eyes between them.

Their presence reminded me of an Eastern gentleman a year before, who, on hearing my background, decided that I was the tail-end of a dying breed. He had made the comment with some solemn nostalgia, with a recall of the romance and dignity of myth. I might have imagined those attributes at the time, but now my imagination was played out. All I could see down the slope was common honesty, that when mixed with those men's souvenirs of pride, would make them laugh at their condition, forget its implications, and guarantee their appearance back out there in the morning. If there had been any calling in that scene I was too close to see it. Calling was of no concern; neither was the name of their vocation, or whether that vocation had centuries or only days to live. I had to grin a little at the Eastern gentleman's badly aimed condolence. But I did appreciate him, at least that afternoon, for throwing me in with such damn fine company.

Focus: Theological Education or Theological Vocation?

J. Louis Martyn

J. Louis Martyn is the Edward Robinson Professor of the New Testament at Union Theological Seminary, New York City. Among other studies, he is the author of *History and Theology in the Fourth Gospel*.

I have to admit being intrigued by that moment when your seat-partner on the airplane finally turns from comments on the weather and select senate committees to ask you, however indirectly, what you "do." Aside from being amused at our habitual assumption that job is the major key to identity ("What's My Line" is one of the longest-lived TV shows), I find that the question nudges me in two directions. On the one hand it sets off in my head a sort of old-style newsreel covering some of the things I have "done," job-wise, in what sometimes seems to amount to two incarnations, one as ditch-digger, truck driver, plumber (not of the Casa Blanca variety), steam-fitter, and engineer, and a second as college and seminary professor. Though I have never carried through with it, I am often tempted to answer the question by reaching back across the divide into one of those earlier "doings," partly, no doubt, because they were done shoulder to shoulder with a simpler, more direct breed of man (Mensch) from whom I am now largely cut off, and in a slower and relatively more put-together world. But I'm not doing those things now (except when the pipes freeze in the cabin), and that relatively intact world seems largely to have moved on.

Hence, on the other hand my seat-mate's question reminds me of the vocational orb in which I currently find myself, the one related to theological education. And being reminded of this vocational orb, I look through my inner window and notice, among other things, some rather threatening thunderheads. It is a truism, of course, to say that theological education in America is in a precarious state of health. Morever, having said as much, we generally turn to matters of curricular design, new degree programs, or reconceived fund-raising campaigns, hoping thereby to find the needed remedy. Yet the illness (is it the Kierkegaardian "Sickness Unto Death"?) hangs on, and the thought begins to settle in that the problems besetting theological education will not be tackled by focusing our attention on theological education. Hence I am intrigued at the possibility of trying to answer my fellow traveler by talking primarily not about theological education, but rather about theological *vocation*. What will it mean, I ask myself, for me to respond by saying that I am *called* to be a professor of theology? That question can be posed for all who teach in seminaries, and I do not think the basic terms of the response would vary a great deal from one seminary setting to another. Yet I have also to be quite specific: What will it mean to respond by saying I am called to be a professor of theology at Union Seminary in the post 1968 years?

I

The Year 1968 Could Have Been a Moment of Truth for Union Seminary

The year 1968 and the location move into the picture, of course, because for me, as for others at Union, the events on Morningside Heights in the spring of that year have proven to be a watershed of a sort that communities encounter only very occasionally. Yet in retrospect it seems that a rather carefully worded sentence is required: The developments from 1968 *could* have been a moment of truth for us at Union, but what was longing to be born has thus far been largely aborted because we failed to accept the eruptions as signs designed to call us back to our corporate *theological*

vocation. It is widely known that the immediate cata-
lyst was provided by the "bust" at Columbia. Some
students there showed quite dramatically their percep-
tivity as regards various aspects of the University's
duplicity and also their anger at being politically disenfranchised within the University's governance structure.
Similar developments ensued at Union, and not without
reason. Our students were also politically disenfranchised. Moreover their insights and opinions had relatively little effect on educational policy. The relative
importance of these two foci—the educational and the
political—was variously evaluated. Some thought the
major problems arose from the fact that the curriculum
was out of whack and needed fixing. Others located the
trouble in the governance system. In any case, there
were two banners behind which the troops gathered:
"Political Enfranchisement for Disenfranchised Groups
(notably students)," and "Educational Innovation."
Only God and the FBI know how many person hours
we spent in governance and curriculum meetings during
the Free University (spring-summer of 1968), through
the Union Commission (1968-69), and into the Assembly and its Councils and Committees (1969-present).
I do not want to be misunderstood. I should say it
again. Students *were* politically disenfranchised and had
little say in educational policy. There was a hierarch-
ically structured character to the community, rather
than either representative or participatory democracy.
And the familiar resistance to change which every institution acquires with venerability was evident in many
ways. Hence it was only with slight reservations that I
myself uttered a word of thanksgiving when student
sensitivity to disenfranchisement got linked up with a
new political savvy and with a certain liberation from

the restraints of politeness and civility in order to tap the obliging reservoir of liberal guilt feelings (not to mention fear) in the seminary's establishment, so as to bring considerable movement toward what was proudly hailed as "student participation in the decision-making processes." Indeed, there is simply no doubt that community-wide participation in the various factors of our common life has not only helped us to avoid mistakes, but has also led us into paths of wisdom we should otherwise have missed.

Yet, for all this, we have to speak, I think, of developments which *could* have added up to a moment of truth—and may yet do so—but which up to the present can scarcely be so characterized. For a funny thing happened on the way toward enfranchisement: We lost our bearings to a considerable extent and consequently found ourselves corporately disheartened. And that happened, one hardly needs to say, not because some "hot-headed" students went off the deep end, but rather because the "revolution" was only skin deep. We dealt with *politics* and with *educational method,* both of which, as our students correctly perceived, are in the same general context. We omitted to deal with the basic issue: *theological vocation.* Hence the skin-deep revolution. For the perceiving of the theological dimensions of the community upheaval is what could have given to the sensitivity for disenfranchisement the truly radical frame of reference it lacked, could have provided the concerns for educational redesign with a fundamental sense of direction which they do not have even now. We lost our way, in short, because we failed to take our bearings solely from what Paul called "The Truth of the Gospel." In the midst of potentially crucial developments the essential ingredient was absent: the fundamental dialectic between the witness of scripture and classical Christian tradition, on the one side, and the fabric of our daily lives, on the other. Rediscovering this dialectic lies, therefore, at the center of what it means to be *called* to be a professor of theology at Union Seminary (or anywhere else). Of course to speak of rediscovering the dialectic can be a way of inviting ourselves to fall into the hybris of those who think they *can* rediscover it. So we need to be clear at the outset that we are talking about the simple process of beginning once again to read the Bible as a community, and of doing that in the sure hope that in his good time God will revivify the dialectic and cause it to overtake us on our way. Let me illustrate, then, by trying to listen simultaneously to Jesus and Paul, on the one hand, and to some of the voices in our seminary community, on the other.

II

JESUS AND UNION SEMINARY:
MARK 10:35FF.

And James and John, the sons of Zebedee, came forward to him and said to him, "Teacher, we want you to . . . grant us to sit, one at your right hand and one at your left, in your glory. . . . And when the ten heard it, they began to be indignant at James and John. And Jesus called them to him and said to them, "You know that those who are supposed to rule over the Gentiles lord it over them, and their great men exercise authority over them. But it shall not be so among you; but whoever would be great among you must be your servant, and whoever would be first among you must be slave of all. For the Son of Man also came not to be served but to serve, and to give his life as a ransom for many."

I recall reading this text in the final communion sermon for the graduating class in the spring of 1968, sensing that we desperately needed to hear it. Yet the recollection is not one that is altogether pleasant because in the ensuing years neither I nor my student and faculty colleagues listened consistently and deeply to these words of Jesus. For if we had, we would have recognized that James and John and the other ten provided portraits of ourselves. Not obvious portraits, of course. None of us openly asked for the chief places. We were, in fact, busily doing away with such marks of hierarchical nonsense. But how? By the politicized means of achieving a balance of powers among the constituent elements of the seminary. Failing to maintain the dialectic by really listening to Jesus' voice, we failed to notice that while we were heavily invested in the "radical" business of moving our community from a quasi-oligarchy to a form of legal democracy, Jesus was speaking not about that movement, but rather about the transition from oligarchy to mutual service (diakonia) in the image of the Son of Man who came not to be served, but to serve.

To have heard Jesus' voice would not have taken us out of politics, of course. He speaks about how things shall be "among you," and that means that he knows quite well there will be among his disciples corporate relationships which are not entirely random. But Jesus' politics, as John Howard Yoder has recently reminded us, are not focused on political enfranchisement. The Man from Nazareth does not instruct his disciples to set up an arrangement in which, by a delicate *balance* of power—various elements in the community eyeing one another carefully in order to maintain *at least* their "fair share" of power ("democratically," of course)—a form of legal democracy can emerge. He speaks rather in a truly radical manner of the Kingdom of *God* in which *God's* hegemony is established over a community marked by *mutual service*. How ironic that a *seminary* "revolution" should usher in as a *new* politics nothing other than the idea of representative democracy! One wonders whether any of us was really studying Greek, so as to ponder the *theological* significance of our passion for demo-cracy (rule by the people), to which corresponded our failure to converse, for example, with the Deuteronomic Historian, who seems to have been overtaken with a passion for ultimate theo-cracy (rule by God) as he formulated his interpretation of the catastrophes experienced by Israel. In short, with the best of (democratic) intentions—said to be excellent pavement—we set about to *govern ourselves* more equitably. I do not speak in this way and in this tone in order to ape the earlier Israelites who, in the Sinai desert, longed to return to a more comfortable bondage in Egypt. Yet it has to be said that in the process of *reducing* the Christian revolution to politicized dimensions, we did not recall the singer of the Philippian hymn (Phil. 2:6-11) who celebrates the eschatological event of God making *Jesus* the absolute Lord. As one colleague has recently remarked, we embarked on a well-intentioned path largely characterized by the fact that we are even now suffering from Christological amnesia. We have managed to forget the verse which we memorized in that youth camp several decades ago: "I have been crucified with Christ; it is no longer I who live, but Christ who lives in me; and the life I now live in the flesh I live by faith in the Son of God, who loved me and gave himself for me" (Gal. 2:20). And forgetting that verse, we have also forgotten that a Christian community lives on "borrowed ego."

I wish it were possible to say that this amnesia and the attendant process of reductionistic politicization leveled off and experienced a reversal a year or so later. On the contrary, we soon learned to move toward good goals via politicized means, leaving the Biblical witness to *God's* Kingdom as a sort of nebulous backdrop not to be taken with utter seriousness. There is not time and space here to chronicle such developments in detail. It will have to suffice to say that our Christological amnesia brought in its wake two remarkable regressions which have further divorced us from our corporate theological vocation.

First, forgetting that a Christian community lives on "borrowed ego," and thus experiencing the upheavals as attacks on *our own* egos, we followed the path of politicization into a regression toward domination by what Paul (instructed a bit by Freud) might have called an Old Age (archaic) super-ego: dependence on man-made law. This regression was hastened by the fact that we (I include myself, of course) did not engage in a communal exegesis of Paul's letter to the Galatians (not to mention chapters 5-8 of his letter to the Romans) *as* we pondered our community responsibilities to those who are the victims of our racist and sexist attitudes. I am in no sense alluding to the abandonment of this exegetical dialectic in order to try to cut the nerve of the community's commitment to Blacks and Women. In fact it is precisely Jesus' proclamation of liberating good news to the poor and oppressed which can give dialectical life to this commitment. However, when the Christological amnesia and the politicization process tempted us toward the formulation of a *nova lex,* we were not in conversation with the Galatians who also understood themselves to be Christians even as they formulated their watchword: "Christ *plus* the law!" Nor were we in conversation with Paul who in Christ painfully discovered the impotence of the law (Rom. 8:3), and who vigorously negated all *additive patterns* as regressions to forms of pre-Christian life. For Christ is, as Paul says, the end of the law (Rom. 10:4). The apostle speaks, therefore, to us when he asks the Galatians how they can turn back again to the weak and beggarly legal frames of reference (Gal. 4:9f.). It remains to be seen whether we shall be able to find a deeply *theological* commitment to Blacks and Women without falling back under the law.

Second, the Christological amnesia made way for some developments toward arrangements in which personal experience threatened to constitute the center and circumference of theological education. Indeed, in some quarters there came a movement toward the uncritical celebration of one's feelings, constituting, in a word, regression toward the dominance of the pleasure principle which rules what Freud called the id. These developments are by no means simple and uniform, and I have no intention of lumping them all together. In certain regards ("Follow your feelings"), however, it does appear that the dialectic with the scriptural witness was notably absent. To be specific, we seem to have steamed ahead on this front without engaging in communal exegesis of the Corinthian correspondence, thereby avoiding conversation with the Corinthians who experimented with their own forms of encounter and sensitivity groups. Nor have we consistently been in conversation with Paul who learned even more clearly in Corinth that the celebration of freedom from law is a liberating event only when the myth of autonomous freedom is broken by an absolute obedience to the Lord whose Body is marked by the mutual "building up" of one another. In this absolute obedience "the discerning of the spirits" is a gift (charisma) which is crucial for the life of the community. For there are many and various ways of saying, "Jesus be cursed!" (I Cor. 12:3).

III

PAUL AND UNION SEMINARY:
I COR. 4:8FF.; II COR. 6:8FF.

All of this brings us face to face with the apostle Paul, and two haunting paragraphs in which he speaks about his sense of theological vocation. I shall quote these momentarily, but first let me say that in rereading them one sees that our Christological amnesia is not surprisingly attended by an eschatological confusion well attested among early Christians. For Paul, theological vocation is the call to engage in the eschatological struggle *at the juncture of the ages.* In contrast to Paul the Galatians wish to avoid that crucial juncture and its struggle by hanging back in allegiance to an additive pattern: Christ plus the old law. They thus live in the Old Age, as though the eschatological drama had not begun. The Corinthians have a different way of avoiding the juncture. They delude themselves into thinking they can leap right over it into a celebration (surprise!) of themselves, assuming an autonomous freedom as their birthright. Paul, on the other hand, finds his theological calling precisely in the eschatological centrality of Jesus' cross which becomes also Paul's

cross in his vocation as an apostle at the end of time.
He thus chides the Corinthians in irony as he says:

Already you are filled! Already you have become
rich! Without us you have become kings! And would
that you did reign, so that we might share the rule with
you! For I think that God has exhibited us apostles as
last of all, like men sentenced to death; because we
have become a spectacle to the world, to angels and
to men. We are fools for Christ's sake, but you are wise
in Christ. We are weak, but you are strong. You are
held in honor, but we in disrepute. To the present hour
we hunger and thirst, we are ill-clad and buffeted and
homeless, and we labor, working with our own hands.
When reviled, we bless; when persecuted, we endure;
when slandered, we try to conciliate; we have become,
and are now, as the refuse of the world, the offscouring
of all things (I Cor. 4:8-13).

The picture Paul employs is in part that of the Roman
circus in which the last act (the eschatological one)
is that of the gladiators who are eventually to die a
public, spectacular death enjoyed by the (cosmic) on-
lookers. In this picture Paul implies that the Corinthians
understand themselves to be safely in the stands, already filled and already rich. By contrast his vocation
places him down on the blood-red sand where the
Two Ages meet and collide in the paradoxical life-giv-
ing cross. The kind of life that God grants is given
nowhere else than in the struggle and daily suffering
and victorious rejoicing at this eschatological turning-
point. That is why Paul says so clearly in the second
of these haunting paragraphs:

We are treated as imposters, and yet are true; as unknown, and yet well known; as dying, and behold we
live; as punished, and yet not killed; as sorrowful, yet
always rejoicing; as poor, yet making many rich; as

having nothing, and yet possessing everything (II Cor. 6:8b-10).

These two paragraphs with their two pictures—painted by a man who served for sometime as a seminary professor (Acts 19:10)—present also *our* theological vocation at the juncture of the ages in our day, a theological vocation focused on God's eschatological struggle to liberate and reconcile all men neither by the law (old or new), nor by a baalistic enthusiasm, but rather in the Body of his Son who came not to be served, but to serve and to give his life for all.

His purpose in dying for all was that men, while still in life, should cease to live for themselves, and should live for him who for their sake died and was raised to life. With us therefore worldly standards have ceased to count in our estimate of any man; even if once they counted in our understanding of Christ, they do so now no longer. When anyone is united to Christ, there is a new world; the old order has gone, and a new order has already begun (II Cor. 5:15-17).

In this new order one finds no competitive (and senseless!) polarity between Christian tradition and personal experience, but rather the dialectic which God is pleased to create between his scriptural witness and the fabric of our contemporary life. The discerning of and immersion in this liberating and humanizing dialectic is what constitutes the eschatological struggle of our theological vocation. And in the struggle the *certainty* of our hope lies in the fact that this theological vocation depends ultimately not on our grasp of it, but rather on God's faithfulness to his promise of life in Jesus Christ. Therefore *this* vocation shall *never* fall to the ground.

Vocation as Grace

Will D. Campbell

Will D. Campbell is director of the Committee of Southern
Churchmen and lives in Mt. Juliet, Tenn.

I got a letter the other day from a man who was a
very close friend of mine twenty years ago. He was a
leader in my first—and last—pastorate. He said that he
was sorry that he had not written during all that time

and that his silence did not mean that he had forgotten me. He said that on the contrary, through mutual friends, he had followed my acrobatics closely over the years.

My *Acrobatics?* My friend has been at the same stand since boyhood. He is a steady workhorse, a successful businessman, a millionaire several times over. I knew that he was really saying to me, "Man, I love you, but why can't you keep a job? Why can't you decide what it is you want to do and do it?"

Well, I guess that is a fair criticism for a man who goes to Sunday School, stays for preaching, makes the Wednesday night prayer meeting, teaches a class, tithes his income, is kind and just to his workers, loves his children, serves on the school board, for surely all that adds up to loving the Lord. In addition he chose what he wanted to do forty years ago and is still at it.

I can claim but one of the above virtues—I do love my children. Some of the others I did do in the past, even equated them at one time or another with Christian witness, but have long since moved along.

At first I was amused by his choice of words to describe my ecclesiastical meanderings. At least I thought I was amused, tried to act amused. But I kept going back to read that letter over and over. It was a long letter and I began to notice that I always paused when I reached that sentence about my acrobatics. And then I began to notice that I stopped there for considerable amounts of time, and finally I began to notice that I got that far in the letter and did not read any further. Then it hit me that his descriptive phrase offended me something awful. So I had to deal with why I was so bugged, so threatened by what a friend had said in all good humor and, I suspected, all seriousness as well.

Of course, I knew at the outset that my analysis would not be a fair and impartial evaluation. I knew that it would be a rationalization, a justification and I knew that I would come out of it looking, at least in my own eyes, presentable for the day of judgment. I knew it because my Daddy and the Bible taught me that much anthropology. But the review began.

Very early in my childhood I decided, or my Mother decided, or my Aunt Susie, or Grandma Bettye, or my Sunday School teacher decided (funny that all those were women) that I would be a preacher. When I was just on the far side of sixteen that decision was consummated one Friday night when a Council composed of my Uncle, my Cousin, my Father, and a country preacher (funny that all those were men) asked me a lot of questions about verbal inspiration of the Scripture, the Virgin Birth, a literal hell, and the Plan of Salvation, and having answered the questions to their satisfaction they declared and decreed that on the following Sunday afternoon that Council would join with the others of the faithful in a ritual setting me apart to the Gospel ministry.

I remember it well. I remember what the preacher said about how many times I would look myself in the mirror and know that I had failed, remember how I knew as I knelt there that it was my Granddaddy's hands as soon as I felt them on my head, how I wondered how long he would stand with those bony, calloused, arthritic fingers pressing down hard, like he was waiting until all the spirit had drained from his own body into mine, how he finally leaned down and touched my head with his lips. And I remember the handtyped document with misspelled words and grammatical errors which was to serve as testament to that event. And I remember how, twenty years later, I would go to great effort and length to find that document, mat it and glue it in a frame covering and forever hiding the degrees and alleged certificates of credentials which had since come my way but which somehow had lost whatever claim to credibility and validity they might have held with me.

That was where the review began. Thirty-one years ago, when I was just a child, I became a preacher. Now an old friend, whose preacher I had once been, referred to me as an acrobat—hardly synonymous with Reverend.

But why did I consider it so demeaning, an affront which more and more seemed to bring under question my very wholeness and probity? The letter had been cordial and in places downright effusive. The man had proved his tolerance by saying nothing of the fact that we had never agreed on any serious issue we had ever discussed, by taking no note of those years when I was active in the Civil Rights Movement while he was active as an ardent segregationist, by ignoring my stand on and participation in the various anti-war activities while the war has his own approval. He could speak of me in warm and glowing terms. But he called me an acrobat!

The review began to make me feel like an old soldier, and while soon I will have passed the half-century mark, my gut considers that I am at life's mid-point, not at its end, ready to fade away.

I recalled that those who sent me forth assumed that I would not stop academically where they had stopped, that I would not even pause or hesitate there. I would, of course, go to college and they would help me; with bath towels and Palmolive soap—which I can

still smell every time I pack to go on a long journey—
with handmade pajamas and linen dresser scarves; with
small checks and little envelopes containing change
from the egg money; with prayers and letters and com-
mendations and congratulations and adulations. But
one day all that would stop. And it would be replaced
with whisperings and unsigned letters, with gossip, and
turning away on occasions of funerals or family visit-
ations which would bring me back home. Some way,
somehow, I had jumped too far. (Jumped? that's what
acrobats do.)

The review revealed that the very thing they had
wanted for me, had insisted that I have, had urged me
into—more and better education—had somehow cut
me off from being their own servant. "He's too good
for us now." "He doesn't speak our language any
more." "He can't preach with the fire and fervor and
spirit he could when he left us." And I knew, though I
denied it, knew even at the time that they were right.
But they had pressed it upon me—"Go to school—get
that education—go to college—go to the finest seminary." They had so urged it and so convinced me that
I followed it to the end of the road, denying, when I
got there, that the road had an end. For the best of
reasons they had bequeathed me an idol. And I had
fallen down and worshipped it. I served it well. And it
stole them away.

Maybe that is why I, one day, covered all the other
documents with the one they had given me. I don't
know. I like to think that my misgivings about the
other documents now are something a little more rational
than that. For I remember wondering even as I was
supping at their table, writing their research papers,
reading their books and listening to their lectures why,

if they knew something about Jesus and the Gospel others did not know, it could be shared only with those of us who were in the top part of the class in high school and who had maintained a steady B average or better in college. I wondered then and I wonder now what is so complicated about that Jesus and that Gospel that those who were alleged to know more than others could not teach it to my brothers and sisters who also wanted to be preachers, in some cases *were* preachers already, but had not done well on Caesar's tests—SAT, CEEB, GRE—or who had failed to see the importance of "a little bit of math, a little bit of science, a little bit of economics, a little bit of physical education" in preparing them for their ministry and had thus done poorly on accumulated quality points. But then, as I said, maybe I'm just still a little bit peeved at them for stealing me away from my people. But to their credit, it wasn't rape. Or, at least it was only statutory.

They had been proud when I "finally quit going to school," as they had begun to put it, when I accepted the pastorate of that acceptable and respectable size Baptist Church in North Louisiana. I believe that I was what they called "a good pastor." I employed the methods some of my teachers had taught me so well. The very first day I was there, even after thirteen hundred miles on the road, I got the names of all those in hospitals and drove another fifty miles to visit them. And even at the time I knew why I was doing it. Not because there were people suffering but because he had said back there that if you always make a point of doing that the first day on the field the word will get around. And that night I went to the church's softball game, volunteered to play centerfield though I knew—

and they soon knew—that I couldn't throw a softball into the infield. But it was to "get the folks to love me" before I started "preaching it to them straight." Why it might have been the least bit important for them to love *me* was a question it didn't occur to me to ask at the time. They had said it was and so I worked at it. And I think I succeeded. I think they did—most of them—come to love me. How many of them came to love the Lord and one another is a different matter.

And instead of the annual five day Vacation Bible School, I organized and directed a summer-long day camp. I thought it was a good one. It was 1952 and so, of course, the day camp was for "our" children, the children who were white. But these people were good people. They did not hesitate to employ a director and pay for a parallel camp for black children, did not even object when we had a few activities together, when we taught them Anti-Defamation League songs like, "You can get good milk from a brown skinned cow, the color of your skin doesn't matter anyhow." And things like that. I joined the civic club and seconded their motions and sang their songs. I went on hunts and overnight hikes. I worked fifteen to twenty hours a week on sermons and became known in the two years I was there as a pretty fair teacher. Or speaker. They called me "our little preacher," gave me regular advances in salary, and paid my medical bills. (That there were those in the community who had no salary at all and who, though dangerously ill, had not seen a doctor in years bothered them not at all and me not enough to refuse it.) But I was no acrobat. I was a preacher, pastoring a church, true to my vows.

Still there was something gnawing away. I did not

really know what it was. I hope now that I left the comfort and security of the steeples because there was just too much unrelated trivia. But I verbalized it then in different ways: "I'm a mascot. I'm fed and housed and patted on the head. I'm paid well, loved and lauded. I'm showed off in front of the other teams. But I'm on a leash. Otherwise it's a great life." Or—and this was most often—I put it in terms of freedom. "There is just no freedom in the pastorate." As if the Christian is ever anything but a prisoner, shouting the good news through the bars as best he can and whenever he can. But I had to have my freedom.

So I went in search of it. It occurred to me that in Divinity School I had majored in what they called Vocational Group D. That was the one called "Religion in Higher Education." It was not to be confused with Group E—"Teaching and Research." That was the one intended for those at the head of the class who would surely go on to graduate schools and become the teachers and deans. Group D was a status rung beneath this but still much better than Group A— "The Parish Ministry." That was for those so obviously dull that they could not possibly be expected ever to do anything else. In Group D one studied Counseling and Group Dynamics, History of the Student Christian Movement, and Social Theory. And, of course, some pretty heady academic things as well because, it was reasoned, if you *really make it* as a Wesley Foundation Director, or B.S.U. or Westminster, or Canterbury Chaplain you will surely be asked to teach a course, or sit in on graduate oral examinations, making you tantamount to faculty member, the very highest of all aspirations.

So I reactivated my vita, on file with a central placement bureau whose responsibility it was to place college chaplains and the like.

There is a very fine country song that begins:

"You followed me to Texas.
    You followed me to Utah.
We didn't find it there,
    So we moved on."

So we did. Me and Brenda, and by now, Penny Elizabeth. On to a sizeable Southern state university where I was to be Director of Religious Life. I had heard of something called "freedom of the pulpit" but knew by then that few took it seriously. I had heard even more of "academic freedom" and assumed at the time that everybody took that seriously. I did not know then that all academic institutions have their own channels of freedom into which all instruction and discussion must fit. Bob Jones may have one channel and Harvard may have another. But a premillennialist would have no more freedom at Harvard than an atheist would at Bob Jones. There is a *line,* seldom announced, sometimes vague and ill-defined, but nevertheless real, which all must follow, and if he doesn't he is soon out, whether by ridicule, tenure denial or outright firing. One may be subtle, the other blatant but the effect is the same. A radical Democrat. A radical Republican. But not an Angela Davis. She doesn't fit within the boundaries. But I didn't know it at the time. So I began to exercise the freedom I had come to claim. It was 1954 and the Supreme Court had just ruled that segregation in public education was illegal. I had long had an interest in race relations, as everybody born and raised in Mississippi had—whether it was good or bad race relations. And knowing while in Divinity School that the Court was sure to rule as it did some southern friends and I had lamented that this issue would be settled before we got back South, had expressed regret that this point of witness would be denied us. Unfortunately we were slightly off the mark. So there I was in the promised land of Academe, where ideas could be expressed, students could be encouraged to provide leadership in their communities, outside speakers at various levels and degrees of radicalism could be imported to jar us all from our lethargy and indifference. Yes, religion could come alive in an atmosphere of liberty and openness and immunity from parish trivia. The Gospel could be proclaimed without restraint, without reining up short in the face of social crises one could spell it out, lay it on the line, say exactly what he meant without fear, without evasion of mind, with no certain toes to be avoided.

Well, not quite. Not so fast, fellow! There were, after all, a few toes to be stepped on lightly, if at all. Don't forget the state legislature is capable of cutting off certain or all appropriations at the slightest provocation. And yes, there is the loyalty oath that you must sign and we all know it's wrong but nobody takes it very seriously. It is, after all, just a little piece of paper. (Saying that in any showdown we will land solidly on the side of Caesar. That we, the faith, the Gospel, the process of education all belong to him and we agree *never* to do anything to subvert him or threaten his domination and ownership of those things. Just a tiny little pinch of incense. Nothing to get one's bowels in an uproar over.) And sure, it is true that we are asked to submit a list of all organizations we have been members of during the past five years but now, really, what does

that have to do with our real mission? Nobody is going
to get fired for belonging to this or that group—though
certainly anyone in his right mind will know better than
to admit to belonging to certain groups known to be
hostile to us. Yes, one guy did get bumped from the
Law School faculty because he had once been a leader
in the ACLU but that was just because a senile old
governor completely misunderstood the purpose and
principle of the ACLU. Certainly none here disapproves
of so mild a movement. And now, for heaven's sake,
let's not make a celebrated case out of the speaker
screening rule. It is just a matter of procedure. If you
want a certain speaker, any speaker, you just turn his
name in to the vice-chancellor. It is nothing more than
clearance to appease those downstate redneck legisla-
tors. True, the vice-chancellor does send the names to
the Americanization Committee of the American Le-
gion but that is just a matter of convenience. It is just
because they have a trustworthy list of subversives and
thus the name submitted will not be subjected to rumor
and gossip. Oh, occasionally they will slip up. Like the
time they confused Lex Miller, the Christian educator
with Lex Miller who works for the ADL of B'nai Brith.
But that was, after all, a natural mistake and no one
got hurt. Now, Son, don't get paranoid just because we
are getting some critical letters about some of the
speakers you are bringing in. You know we're with
you. Of course, we would have to agree that maybe
you are stacking the deck a bit. After all, there is something to talk about in convocations besides race and
desegregation. And that Episcopal guy from Ohio who
won all that money on the quiz show and then gave it
to the NAACP. Surely you will admit that we had no
choice but to cancel his engagement. He was nothing

but a troublemaker. It was the Willie Magee case all over again. It was the communist trying to be the Director of Religious Life. Sometimes you just don't seem to understand. Like the time you went down there to visit those people at that communal farm in the Delta. Just because their State Senator called up here next day and asked what the hell one of our men was doing in his county doesn't mean that we are moving into some sort of fascist state or concentration camp as you seem to imply. Yes, sometimes you just don't seem to understand. The mark of an educated man is to have the capacity to adjust. Maybe you're a bit overzealous. But don't think we're not with you. This is just not the ditch to die in and when the time comes for you to go it will be time for all of us to go, and we'll all walk across that bridge together. But right now we've all got a quick job of educating to do and Rome wasn't built in a day. No, we don't know who dumped all those black and white ping-pong balls on your lawn the night after you were caught playing ping-pong with a Negro friend of yours, but you *must* have known that it was poor judgment to have him on the campus with you in the first place. We tried to make that clear after Carl Rowan spent the night at your house. Of course, we were clean on that one and told the Sovereignty Commission who investigated you that it was your house and not university property and there was nothing we could do. Certainly you have a right to have anyone you wish in your own home. But whether it is good judgment is a different matter. No, we can't find out who put the cup of feces in the punch bowl at the reception for new students. It was a nasty thing to do and if we knew who did it he wouldn't be on this campus five minutes. But, of course, we can't find out! We did, however, check with the medical school and unless the person had amoebic dysentery or something like that there was no danger to anyone's health. Well, yes there is the matter of esthetics but we're with you, man. And we'll defend academic freedom to the last man and to the last dollar of appropriation. But we're not talking here about academic freedom. This is just not the ditch to die in and we'll all go together when the time comes.

> "We didn't find it there,
>   So we moved on."

The National Council of Churches was looking for someone to set up an office in the South and work full time in race relations. Lady luck was smiling big for us. What could be more ideal, more challenging, more satisfying and fulfilling? Where was there a greater potential for MINISTRY, for proclaiming the Gospel, no longer in a vacuum but in the face of a real flesh and blood, life and death situation? So me and Brenda and Penny Elizabeth, and by now, Bonnie Ruth, moved on. Free at last! Now I can be a preacher!

From the restrictions and phony issues of the parish to the assumed enlightenment of the university might have been a long journey. But it wasn't. I found there was absolutely no difference between the two. The organization was the same, the goals, the pitfalls, the snares, the tares—it was all the same. Now I was going to the most "liberal" of all ecclesiastical organizations. Here it is. Here is the freedom ball. Take it and run with it. It's your set of downs, first and goal. Boogedy, boogedy, here I come, ready or not, all eyes open.

The pastorate had lasted a little over two years. The university had lasted the same length of time, almost to the day. My vocation seemed to be in multiples of two.

For the job with the Council was funded for two years, no promises made after that. So I had two years to desegregate the South. And in those days a lot of us thought in those terms. The hard-headed realists would sometimes speak in terms of five, maybe even ten years before the job would be complete but not the romantics among us.

And it was quite a period—that two years of '56-'58. It was watching a significant social movement born and grow into adulthood. It was being the only white man at the formation of the Southern Christian Leadership Conference. Go visit with the preachers of Clinton, Tennessee, with the whole town under a virtual state of seige with leadership provided by a demagogue named John Kasper. There was Paul Turner, the First Baptist man, the least likely of the group, saying little and promising nothing, but next week going to school with the Negro children and getting himself beaten half to death. It was flying off to Little Rock and facing Mr. Faubas' troops, and sitting at night with the mothers and fathers of those nine courageous black children, and walking to the schoolhouse with them next morning. Back to Nashville where the celebrated "Nashville Plan" would admit nine black children to the first grade. Then next year they would be in the second grade while some new ones would be in the first and so on until grade twelve. There were the riots over that, and there was the trial of John Kasper, and the feeling that justice had been done when he was sent to prison. New Orleans, Montgomery, Birmingham, Baton Rouge, Chattanooga, Fort Worth, Richmond, every town and every city was a battleground. There was a lot of action, a lot of savage violence, a lot of things I had never witnessed before and witnessed now only as one more white onlooker. But I was there. The Civil Rights Movement has been reviewed enough times. The heroic names have been called. I will not do it here. My own role was minor. My only claim can be that I was there as it was happening and I doubt if that has much to do with vocation. And it is of that we are trying here to speak.

The two years ended and we were refunded. And the crises continued. It was largely a matter of just going out, day after day, not really knowing where, and not always knowing why. And maybe that is all vocation is. Ever. Those who employed me did not know what to tell me to do. And I didn't know what to do. I just sort of reveled in the freedom. But

> "Freedom's just another word
> for nothing left to lose."

We began to have our troubles and our differences. They, and no doubt I, began to assume that we did know what to do. We began to organize and institutionalize the freedom. Exit freedom. There was the now famous Chicago Conference on Religion and Race in 1962. It was to be the one to end all conferences on the subject. There was my prepared text to that conference in which one sentence said that if I live to be as old as my father I expected to see white people killed by black people in the same manner as black people had been killed by whites. "If black people are equally good, then they are equally bad," I reasoned. There was the challenge to my right to say that at the conference. "Well, that's what I believe." "Well, *believe* it back in Tennessee, but don't *say* it in Chicago." Then came the mounting pressures and misunderstandings as the institutionalizing process continued. A national magazine carried an account I had written of some ministers and rabbis arrested and jailed in Albany, Georgia. The article was interpreted as being sympathetic with the redneck sheriff. And it was, though there is a difference between sympathy and agreement. So now I was expected to submit all articles and speeches to New York. "Just for clearance. Just to keep communication open between us." Of course I refused. No one had asked me to do that when I worked for the state of Mississippi and I would not do it for what was supposed to be the most liberal and free religious organization in the nation.

But some things began to come clear to me. It was not really freedom I had been seeking at all. What I had been seeking was a home, acceptance, community. By now I had discovered that freedom is not something that you find or someone gives to you. It is something you assume. And then you wait for someone to come and take it away from you. And the amount of resistance you put up is the amount of freedom you will have. It began to be clear to me that *all* institutions, every last one of them, no matter the claim, no matter the purpose, no matter the stated goals, all of them exist for their own selves, all of them look out for their own interest first, are self-loving, self-concerned, self-regarding, self-preserving, and thus are inherently evil. All of them. For example, I thought for a time that my experience at a southern state university was unique. But that was before a dean in an Ivy League university told me that student strikes against Dow Chemical could not be tolerated because you can't operate a university in the midst of chaos. And before I saw numerous of the schools known for their enlightenment and liberalism respond to ROTC affiliation by no longer giving aca-

demic credit for it. "We'll continue to teach killing but
we wash our hands in the Pilate basin of Academe."
(Every bomb dropped should carry a tag bearing the
good news to the victims that no academic credit was
awarded on its behalf.) And I thought for a time that
my experience at a Louisiana Baptist Church was
unique. But that was before the pastor of a liberal and
fashionable United Church in Massachusetts, located
on what is reported to be the richest residential street
in the world, built with slave and rum money, complained that his major problem was that one of his eight
ushers refused to wear the morning cutaway like the
others did. This unhappy event was reported in the
midst of a stinging indictment of southern churches for
doing nothing in the racial crisis. So now I know that
my own experiences should not be read as caricatures
of the others. And the relating of those experiences
should not be read as criticism of specific institutions
or organizations. The goals and purposes of a major
religious organization may be stated differently from the
goals and purposes of a major insurance company. But
the organization which makes them go is always the
same and thus the goals and purposes *become* the same,
no matter how stated—the perpetuation of the institution.

> "We didn't find it there,
>   So we moved on."

Me and Brenda, and Penny Elizabeth, and Bonnie
Ruth, and by now, Lee Webb. On to this small, rocky
Tennessee farm and a little front thing called the Committee of Southern Churchmen. It is a number of different things. It is this magazine and it is a cabin adjacent
to the residence which serves as mini-folk school, half-

way house, guest house, hide away for people to meet, talk, plan, visit, study, write books or, more importantly, rest. It is this log house office where there are more weddings, funerals, baptisms, setting folks aside to the Gospel ministry, crying with folks with personal problems (we used to call it counseling) than there ever was when I served the steeples or related structures. Why that is true I do not know. It is a few dozen men and women, Roman to Pentecostal, who believe that the Gospel has to do with poor folks, black folks, drug folks, prison folks, military deserter folks, Ku Klux Klan folks and others of God's children. Still folks want to know, "But what do you *do?*" The others can answer for themselves. As for me I still do pretty much what I have done since that summer afternoon in 1941 when Grandpa Bunt placed his worn and calloused hands on my head, thus setting me apart to the Gospel ministry. For I'm a preacher.

But it has also become clear to me that what I *do* is not the point of vocation. It has, in the course of this mid-point review of my ministry become clear to me that my friend is right. I *am* an acrobat. Praise the Lord! That's all I know how to do. Just jump and hop and somersault around, hoping occasionally to be in the right place at the right time. For vocation is an illusive and elusive thing. Maybe the only way to ever have it is to quit looking for it. In my university ministry days I used to go to a lot of conferences. A lot of them had the same theme for the late adolescent students—"WHO AM I?" Well, Jesus answered that question a long time ago. If you want to find out who you are, he said, forget the question. If you want to find yourself, then lose yourself and quit all the navel gazing on so silly a question as who you are. I know who I am. I'm Will Campbell. Beyond that I don't care. Maybe it is the same with vocation. For maybe it is never *my* vocation. It used to bother me that I couldn't have faith when they told me I was saved by faith. Then I learned it was the *faith*fulness of God and not my faith that saved me. Then it bothered me when they told me I had to have a vocation to reflect or complement that act of God. If the faith is not mine then perhaps the vocation is not mine. "What am I going to do with my life?" St. Paul said we are earthen vessels. And that is all he said about vocation. If Jesus is Lord, then He is Lord of what happens in, through, because of, and to me. What I do to make a living may simply be my own business, of no concern to the Lord. What He does with me, through me, with no choosing on my part, no help from me, no planning, strategizing, scheming, next stepping may be no business or no concern of mine.

Once my Grandma Bettye got a new plaid flannel bathrobe for Christmas. It was a present from her son in another state who worked for the government and who, we all assumed at the time, had lots of money. It was red and green with black stripes dividing the colorful squares. The very first Sunday after Christmas my Grandma wore it to the meeting. She sat right up on the front row of the section that ran perpendicular to the pulpit. It was where all the older women sat, along with the middlesized grandchildren—those who no longer had to sit with Mamma but had not yet discovered that it was more fun to sit in the back and sing parodies on the hymns to impress the girls, or carve their initials on the pews during the sermon. Some of the more sophisticated of Grandma's daughters-in-law were embarrassed and had some rather caustic things to say to Grandma for wearing a bathrobe to church. But Grandma Bettye handled it well. "Just hush. It's the prettiest thing I have ever seen and the Lord deserves the best." And she added, "Anyway, I ain't got no bathroom." It was the middle of the depression. Maybe that's all vocation is. But the moral of the story is not just that Grandma showed off the prettiest thing she had to Jesus. That is part of it. But the real moral is that the pretty thing she showed off to Jesus had been given to her. It was a matter of grace.

Well, thank you, brother, for calling me an acrobat. It was not such an insult after all. For I have seen them high on that wire, standing on tiptoes, jumping, flipping, turning, leaning this way and that, never trusting their own skills and strength alone to catch them for there is always the team around. And as soon as that evening's performance is over they are always ready to move on to the next town. It is an elusive thing for them too, an elusive dream and scheme, always somewhere else, always beckoning them on, only to find that it isn't at the next performance either, never becoming a reality, always a driving, pushing, haunting upper that keeps them jumping, walking on tippytoes, swinging and somersaulting high over the crowd at Municipal Auditorium —God's world.

Long before the process of my vocational self-examination (justification) began I once cornered and talked to a high wire artist in a small traveling circus. I asked him why he chose that particular way of making a living. The first few minutes were filled with circus romance—the thrill of hurling through space, feeling at the last instant that pasty flesh of two always welcomed hands pressing around the wrists, swinging you forward to the next set of pasty hands which in turn deliver you safely back to the starting platform; the joy of laughter

and approval and applause in the eyes of "children of
all ages," the clanking of train wheels moving you on
to the next city; even the part about it being a comfortable life with good pay. But finally he said what I had
not expected him to say. "Now you really want to know
why I go up there on that damned thing night after
night after night?" I said I did. "Man, I would have
quit it a long time ago. But my sister is up there. And
my wife and my father are up there. My sister has more
troubles than Job. My wife is a devil-may-care nut and
my old man is getting older. If I wasn't up there, some
bad night, man . . . smash!" His foot stomped the floor
with a bone cracking thud.

"H'mmm."

He started to walk away but I had one more question to ask and ran after him. "But why do *they* stay up
there?" He looked like he didn't want to answer, wasn't
going to answer. But then he did. Turning from the door
of the boy's locker room in the county seat high school,
with a brown craft cardboard box and heavy crayola
sign: MEN'S COSTUMES above it for the evening's
performance, he looked me up and down and then, as
he disappeared, blurted it out: "Because I drink too
much!"